ARIZONA

ART OF THE STATE

ART OF THE STATE

ARIZONA

The Spirit of America

Text by Cynthia Bix

Harry N. Abrams, Inc., Publishers

NEW YORK

This book was prepared for publication at
Walking Stick Press, San Francisco

Project staff:
    Series Designer: Linda Herman
    Series Editor: Diana Landau

For Harry N. Abrams, Inc.:
    Series Editor: Ruth A. Peltason

Page 1: Horse with birds, cardboard cutout by Mamie Deschilles, 1990. *Collection Patrick Eddington. Photo Susan Makov*

Page 2: *Cathedral Rock* by Eugene Berman, 1950–1963. *Phoenix Art Museum*

Library of Congress Cataloguing-in-Publication Data
Bix, Cynthia Overbeck.
    Arizona : the spirit of America, state by state / text by Cynthia Bix.
        p.   cm. — (Art of the state)
    Includes bibliographical references and index.
    ISBN 0–8109–5555–5 (hardcover)
    1. Arizona—Miscellanea.   I. Title.   II. Series.
F811.B59   1998
979.1—dc21   98–3990

 Harry N. Abrams, Inc.
100 Fifth Avenue
New York, N.Y. 10011
www.abramsbooks.com

Animal Keeper II by Linda Lomahaftewa, 1990. *Courtesy the artist*

CONTENTS

"Arizona. Mellow, golden, sustaining,
beautiful, clean with desert wind…I tell you…
this…is a wonderful country."

Zane Grey, Lost Pueblo, *1927*

A land of spectacular beauty; a land that challenges all living things yet holds out the constant promise of inspiration; a land where human endeavor strives to match nature's grandest works—Arizona is, indeed, a "wonderful country."

Roofed with an endless sky above a landscape of wrinkled and sculpted rock, Arizona leaves a potent impression on the senses. At its benign best, it beguiles and inspires with golden light; dry, clean desert air; and stirring vistas. At its most ferocious, it assaults with searing heat, dust, and wind blowing across barren wastes.

A many-faceted place, Arizona refuses to conform to the stereotypes it evokes—the red-desert backdrop hung with cactus and mesa, familiar from countless movie and TV renditions. Much of the state indeed is desert—mile upon mile of dry, rocky land. Yet even here there is remarkable variety and abundant life. That memorable symbol, the many-armed saguaro cactus, is but one life form in one kind of desert. Other desert environments are characterized by looming mesas and rock spires, or by ever-shifting sand dunes, populated by snakes and scorpions or dotted with creosote bushes. Also rising above Arizona's deserts are mountains, dramatic and lushly forested, snow-capped in winter. Then there are Arizona's canyons—dramatic gashes in the earth that

The Chasm of the Colorado by Thomas Moran, 1873–74. *National Museum of American Art/Art Resource*

enfold between their rocky cliffs mighty rivers, mysterious pueblo ruins, and a collection of plants and animals all their own. The greatest of these, the Grand Canyon, is the most stupendous example in a land with an embarrassment of such riches.

The character of this fascinating state is also the character of its people; tough, resilient, full of spice, endlessly varied, and often unpredictable. The original inhabitants—the Navajo and the Hopi, the Tohono O'odham and

Jackrabbit Trading Post sign on Route 66. *Richard Sisk/Panoramic Images. Opposite: The Rattlesnake by Frederic Remington, 1905. Frederic Remington Art Museum, Ogdensburg, New York*

the Apache—have tenaciously and inventively lived on this challenging land for centuries. The Mexicans, relative newcomers, brought with them to Arizona a rich culture long adapted to dryland ways. The most recent immigrants, the Anglos, have added to the mix a seasoning of cultures from Europe and "back East," as well as their own special brand of pioneering spirit.

People who encounter Arizona can't help but have strong responses to its physical marvels and demands. For many, that response has found voice in arts and crafts, literature and song. Native American art—clay pottery, weavings from sheep's wool, paintings composed of sand—comes literally from the land, while religious chants and rituals are linked directly to the cycle of the seasons. Mexican-American arts, including culinary art, make use of what can be coaxed from the earth—chiles, corn, and beans for an endlessly creative cuisine; metalwork crafted with native ore; and, of course, the culture and cult of the cowboy—originally the Mexican *vaquero*. Springing from a life lived outdoors, in all weathers, the best of cowboy art and song expresses an intimacy with wind and rain, dust and sun, and endless miles of lonely country.

In more recent times, people have striven to tame Arizona's deserts—with dams on the rivers and canals through the deserts, in boomtowns replete with air conditioning and high-rises. To an extent they've succeeded:

agriculture now flourishes, and a lush resort life awaits those who escape snowbound winters to Arizona. But many residents, both old and new, feel a kinship with the desert and seek ways to live with the land as it is. This impulse toward harmony between humans and a demanding yet rewarding environment has been expressed again and again in art and architecture. Architects are inspired to make their designs look and feel like an integral part of the landscape; painters, sculptors, filmmakers, and writers alike celebrate what is unique and beautiful about the setting and try to capture it on canvas, film, and the page.

The youngest state in the lower 48, Arizona has all the confidence, brashness, and lively charm of youth. It's a place where people are still experimenting, still trying things on for size. The state's traditional heritage —that of Native Americans and Hispanics, and of the rough-and-ready Old West—is always being combined and recombined with contemporary trends, from New Age ideas to resort styles. Urbanites and Sun Belt retirees, ranchers and artists live side by side amid scenes of awe-inspiring natural grandeur. Arizona is primeval and postmodern, Old West and New Age, all rolled into one. ☽

"THE GRAND CANYON IS TO THE SOUTHWEST AS THE Mona Lisa is to the Louvre—an international landmark for an otherwise fabulous collection."

Michael Grant, American Southwest, 1992

ARIZONA

"Grand Canyon State"
"Copper State"
48th State

Date of Statehood
FEBRUARY 14, 1912

Capital
PHOENIX

Bird
CACTUS WREN

Flower
SAGUARO CACTUS BLOSSOM

Tree
PALOVERDE

Gemstone
TURQUOISE

Mammal
RING-TAILED CAT

Reptile
RIDGE-NOSED RATTLESNAKE

Fossil
PETRIFIED WOOD

"Ditat Deus" (God Enriches)

State motto

The symbols Arizonans have chosen for their state celebrate two kinds of riches bestowed on it: its natural wealth of desert plants, animals, and golden sunshine, and the wealth found by humans—ore from the earth, vast tracts of rangeland, and fertile soil

Cactus wren and saguaro blossom

from which irrigation coaxes abundant crops. Arizona's emblems announce the youthful energy of an economy on the move. Against the flag's blue field and setting-sun motif, a copper star shines for mineral wealth. The seal features the state's earliest enterprises—water reclamation, ranching, and mining. Arizona's state flora and fauna denote the desert's beauty and fecundity: the paloverde with its yellow springtime blossoms, and the big, milky-white

bloom of the saguaro. Flora in its petrified form is the state fossil. In desert country, it's only right to have a state reptile; Arizona's is the ridge-nosed rattlesnake. The petite cactus wren is a creature of the desert, too, nesting among the spines of the cholla cactus. ☽

The Devil was given permission one day
To select him a land for his own special way;
So he hunted around for a month or more
And fussed and fumed and terribly swore,
But at last was delighted a country to view
Where the prickly pear and the mesquite grew
And now, no doubt, in some corner of hell
He gloats over the work he has done so well,
And vows that Arizona cannot be beat
For scorpions, tarantulas, snakes, and heat....

Charles O. Brown,
"Arizona: The Land That God Forgot," 1879

Above: In spring, the state tree—paloverde—lights up the desert with its clouds of yellow blossoms. It shares the stage with saguaro and mesquite, wild poppies and mustard blossoms. *Photo Charlie Ott. Below:* Vintage shipping tag from the Petrified Forest. *Wallis Collection*

Above: Door handle in form of a rattlesnake on 200-year-old mesquite doors at the San Xavier del Bac Mission. *Photo Edward McCain Opposite below:* Turquoise, the state gemstone, may be sky-blue or green-hued, clear or richly veined. It's used most notably in Navajo and Zuni jewelry-making. *Photo Researchers, Inc.*

OLD FAITHFUL
PETRIFIED LOG IN ARIZONAS
WORLD FAMOUS PETRIFIED FOREST.
COPYRIGHTED — DISTRIBUTED BY BUCK LEE CO. — HOLBROOK, ARIZ.

Rattlesnake Chili

1-2 lbs. ground rattlesnake, armadillo, or chicken

1 med. onion, chopped

3 cloves garlic, minced

2 6-oz. cans tomato puree

1 tbsp. ground cumin

Half a 12-oz. can of beer

2 4-oz. cans diced green chiles

4 tbsp. ground red chiles or chili powder

Salt and pepper to taste

Optional: 2 16-oz. cans pinto beans

In skillet, brown ground meat with onion and garlic. Put in large pot or electric slow-cooker; add remaining ingredients. In pot: bring to boil, then reduce heat and simmer 45 minutes to 1 hour. In slow-cooker: cook 6 hours or over-night on low setting. Serves 6.

Adapted from Patricia Myers's recipe in Arizona Highways

Above: Bola tie with inlaid corn motif by Hopi jeweler Bernard Dawahoya. *Photo Jerry Jacka*
Right: Dedicated in 1901, the State Capitol in Phoenix is topped by "Winged Victory," a weather-vane in female form. *Photo Tom Bean/DRK Photo*

Bola! Bola!

Arizona is the only state to have official neckwear. In this distinctly Western culture, where many consider neckties *de trop,* the bola tie was once *de rigueur.* Named after the Argentine gaucho's *baleadora,* or "throwing cord," it's a loop of woven leather tightened by a sliding clasp, usually native silver and often adorned with turquoise, the state gem. Not everyone thinks highly of the bola; Arizona novelist Ray Ring derides it as "so goofy most wives won't let their husbands appear in one." Nor can everyone agree on the spelling: *bola* versus *bolo.*

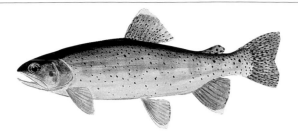

"Arizona March Song"

Come to this land of sunshine
To this land where life is young.
Where the wide, wide world is waiting,
The songs that will now be sung.
Where the golden sun is flaming
Into warm, white, shining day,
And the songs of men are blazing
Their priceless right of way.

Sing the song that's in your hearts
Sing of the great Southwest,
Thank God, for Arizona
In splendid sunshine dressed.
For thy beauty and thy grandeur,
For thy regal robes so sheen
We hail thee Arizona
Our Goddess and our queen.

*This martial anthem (words by Margaret Rowe
Clifford and music by Maurice Blumenthal)
was named the state song in 1919. In 1982
legislators chose as an "alternate" the more
folksy, laid-back "Arizona" by Rex Allen, Jr.
("Ooh, Arizona/You're the magic in me.")*

Whence "Arizona"?

Scholars think the name Arizona comes from Native American words, but they disagree about which ones. It may be from the Tohono O'odham (Papago) *arizonac* or *aleh-zon,* meaning "little spring," or from the ancient Aztec word *arizuma,* meaning "silver bearing." Both apply.

Top: Apache Trout by James Prosek. This threatened species (*Oncorhynchus gilae apache*) is considered sacred by the White Mountain Apache, who help to manage its reduced numbers. *Courtesy the artist. Above:* Many a tourist has succumbed to the appeal of a snow globe; this one, proudly displaying the state's nickname, may have come from one of Arizona's ubiquitous trading posts. *Photo David Emerick*

A.D. 450–800 Anasazi and Hohokam cultures flourish.

1540 Coronado's expedition of conquest extends into Arizona, which he claims for Spain.

1692 Jesuit Father Eusebio Francisco Kino establishes missions in southern Arizona.

1751 Pima and Papago tribes expel Spanish priests and miners.

1753 Spanish soldiers establish first *presidio* at Tubac; Jesuit priests return to Arizona.

1797 Mission San Xavier del Bac is completed.

1821 Mexico wins independence from Spain; establishes Territory of Nuevo Mexico, which includes New Mexico and Arizona.

1824 Anglo traders and trappers arrive.

1846 The Mexican War is declared by the U.S.; General Stephen Watts Kearny leads the Army of the West through Arizona toward California.

1847 The Mormon Battalion, led by Lt. Col. Philip St. George Cooke, traverses Arizona, forging the first wagon road from Santa Fe, New Mexico, to the Pacific.

1848 Mexican War ends; under the Treaty of Guadalupe Hidalgo, Mexico cedes to the U.S. most of Arizona.

1853 The U.S. acquires from Mexico the land between the Gila River and the southern boundary of Arizona as a result of the Gadsden Purchase.

1853 and 1857–58 Railroad surveys are made, by Edward F. Beale, using camels for pack animals.

1857–58 First mail routes open up.

1858 Gold is discovered near Gila City.

1861–62 Chiricahua Apaches fight with U.S. Army troops.

1863 U.S. government creates Arizona Territory.

1869 Major John Wesley Powell explores the Grand Canyon. Population: 9,658.

1871–86 Fighting between Apaches and U.S. Army; Geronimo surrenders in 1886.

1877 Silver is discovered near Tombstone.

1880 The first railroad service reaches Tucson; copper mining begins in Bisbee.

1881 Gunfight at the O.K. Corral.

1883 Transcontinental railroad crosses through northern Arizona.

1889 Arizona's territorial capital is moved from Prescott to Phoenix.

1904 The Kolb brothers build their famous photographic studio on the rim of the Grand Canyon.

1911 Construction of Theodore Roosevelt Dam completed.

1912 Arizona is granted statehood on February 14. Novelist Willa Cather visits Arizona; *The Song of the Lark* reflects her impressions.

1920 Western novelist Zane Grey builds a cabin near Payson. Population: 334,162.

1920s Author Oliver La Farge visits Arizona; his resulting novel about the Navajo, *Laughing Boy,* wins a Pulitzer Prize.

1928 The Tucson Symphony Orchestra is founded.

1929 The Heard Museum, devoted to Native American art, is founded in Phoenix.

1930 The Coolidge Dam is completed; the discovery of the planet Pluto is reported from Flagstaff's Lowell Observatory.

1935 British novelist J. B. Priestly visits Arizona; records his visit in the book, *Midnight on the Desert.*

1936 Hoover Dam is completed.

1937 Frank Lloyd Wright establishes his Taliesin West at Scottsdale.

1939 Painter Maynard Dixon settles in Tucson.

1939 Old Tucson Studios is built for the filming of the Western classic *Arizona.*

1946 Painter Max Ernst arrives in Sedona.

1948 Native Americans on reservations are finally granted voting rights.

1963 Glen Canyon Dam is completed.

1965 The Cowboy Artists of America is founded in Sedona.

1966 Colin Fletcher completes first solo hike through the Grand Canyon; records his experience in *The Man Who Walked Through Time.*

1967 Arizona Theatre Company is founded in Tucson.

1980 Population: 2,718,425.

1981 Arizonan Sandra Day O'Connor becomes the first woman appointed to the U.S. Supreme Court.

1982 First annual Jazz on the Rocks festival in Sedona.

1990 Restoration work is done on Mission San Xavier del Bac.

1991 Arizona River Project completed, bringing Colorado River water to Phoenix and Tucson. Central Arizona Project (for irrigation) is completed.

1995 Population surpasses 4,000,000.

Ajo Range, Organ Pipe Cactus National Monument. Here, where three deserts meet, mountains form a backdrop for stunning native flora, such as the giant saguaro cactus of the Sonoran Desert and the organ pipe cactus. *Photo Carr Clifton. Below: Stages of Bloom* by Ed Mell, 1996. Illustrator and landscape artist Mell first gained notice in New York for his arresting commercial art before returning to his native Arizona. *Suzanne Brown Galleries, Scottsdale*

Arizona's landscape is no place for people who think small. It's big, wide-open country—grand in scale—slashed with enormous canyons, rising into mountains and mesas, and leveling out into vast desert expanses. Also vast is the record of time it represents. This land lays bare the slow work of geologic time, stretching back millions of years, in which mountains have risen, seas have receded, and the earth has been carved by wind and water into deep canyons and fantastic rock formations.

For simplicity's sake, picture the state as three main regions—the desert, the mountains, and the Colorado Plateau (high, broken tableland cut by canyons and studded with distinctive buttes and mesas). Rivers—the Colorado, the Little

Colorado, the Gila, and their tributaries—flow among these regions like connecting threads, carrying precious water from the high country. Each region offers its expected sights—the red mesas of cowboy movies, saguaros framed on the far horizon—but surprises abound. The mountains beckon with cool, moist pine forests; the desert becomes a spring garden of flowers; and parched canyon beds roar to life with the waters of a flash flood. 🐾

Grand Canyon by Edward H. Potthast, c. 1910. Potthast first came to Arizona by train in 1910 with Thomas Moran and several other artists to paint the Grand Canyon's splendors. The bright palette of this canvas links the painter with the American Impressionists. *The Anschutz Collection*

Pattern of sand dunes, Canyon de Chelly National Park. The soft forms of the dunes have been described by architectural historian Reyner Banham as "a horizon made of reclining figures by Henry Moore." *Photo Robert Frerk. Below:* The desert collared lizard. *Photo John Gerlach Opposite above:* Giant saguaros, Saguaro National Monument. *Photo James Randklev Opposite below: Chain of Spires Along the Gila River* by John Mix Stanley, 1855. As expedition artist for General Stephen Kearny in 1846, Stanley made on-the-spot sketches, later transformed into this romanticized painting. *Phoenix Art Museum*

Desert Light, Desert Life

The word "desert" doesn't begin to explain the complexities of Arizona's definitive bioregion. There are really four major desert environments (all spill over into neighboring states and Mexico). They are the Sonoran, the Great Basin (or Painted), the Mojave, and the Chihuahuan Deserts—each with its distinctive climate, scenery, and flora and fauna. With an annual rainfall of up to 11 inches in some places, the Sonoran Desert is hospitable, as deserts go. It's home to a rich assortment of plants and animals, including the saguaro cactus and paloverde tree, the coyote, and numerous snakes and lizards. The Mojave Desert, on Arizona's northwestern border, is an inland ocean of sand. The gigantic, rocky landscape of the Great Basin and the flat, featureless *playa* of the Chihuahuan Desert round out the range of Arizona's deserts.

"YOU ARE SHUT IN BY DISTANCES OF LIGHT. YOU WALK in the focus of the sun's rays. You are clothed in sun; sun glows in your blood, until even your bones feel incandescent. You feel in your body why the desert wears grey, and why it blooms with such vital brilliance."

Nancy Newhall, in Arizona Highways, *January 1954*

"...WHAT APPEAR TO BE MEMBERS OF AN ALIEN RACE are standing all over the basin, caught standing in the middle of arrested gestures of affirmation, command, supplication, welcome, repulsion...the limbs of the saguaro demand to be read as living gestures."

Reyner Banham, Scenes in America Deserta, *1982*

Along the edges of Arizona's deserts rise lofty, far-off shapes of dark blue or purple or red, like gigantic stage backdrops. Biologists call these mountains "sky islands." High on their slopes exists a world as different from the surrounding ocean of desert as an island is from the sea. In their cool, moist climate, forests of pine, aspen, fir, and spruce flourish—home to bighorn sheep, squirrels, black bears, and other high-country creatures. Winter frosts the peaks with sparkling snow, an unexpected delight in a mostly hot, dry state. The mountains gather clouds that bring life-giving rain, transforming the desert into a place of plenty. Native Americans have known this for centuries; their ceremonial calendars revolve around the cycle of rain and drought; songs and chants celebrate thunder and rain-clouds. Spirits dwell in these holy mountains, especially atop Mount Humphreys (at 12,633 feet, Arizona's highest peak). Long before it received its English name, the Navajo called it "Dook'o'ooslid"; the Hopi, "Nuvatukyaovi"—home of the kachina spirits. ❧

Above: Desert bighorn ram. Herds of these majestic sheep once roamed Arizona's high country; human encroachment has restricted their territory. *Photo Tom Bean/DRK Photo. Right: The Super-stitions by Ed Mell, 1997. Private collection*

Opposite above: Fog drifts over a forest of ponderosa pines in the White Mountains, near Hannagan Meadow. The world's largest stand of ponderosas grows in northern Arizona's mountains, along the beautiful Mogollon Rim. *Photo Edward McCain*

A cloud on top of Evergreen Mountain
is singing,
A cloud on top of Evergreen Mountain is
standing still.
It is raining and thundering up there,
It is raining here.
Under the mountain the corn tassels are shaking,
Under the mountain the slender spikes
of child corn are glistening.

Apache

Canyon Country

Here is a starkly beautiful, grandiose land of rock, sculpted over eons by wind and water, scoured and sun-baked into

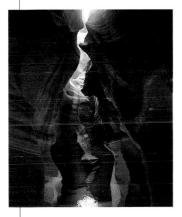

deep canyons, soaring spires, and flat mesas that plunge abruptly thousands of feet. Much of Arizona's canyon country, including the Grand Canyon, lies on the Colorado Plateau, which covers large parts of Arizona, New Mexico, Colorado, and Utah; its countless canyons and mesas are sliced by the Colorado River and its tributaries. Arizona's canyons can be dramatic, like Canyon de Chelly and Paria Canyon—in places 1,100 feet deep and only 10 feet wide. They can be refuges of light and color, like Sedona's Oak Creek Canyon in autumn, bright with turning oak and sumac, or strange and forbidding, dark and deep. Canyon de Chelly—the name

comes from *Tsegi*, meaning "rock canyon" in Navajo—is enclosed within sheer sandstone walls 1,000 feet high. The rock is streaked and flaked, marked with the record of 165 million years. It has been home to humans for a much shorter time—nearly 2,000 years; ancient dwellings carved into its walls attest to civilizations gone by. Today it's part of the huge Navajo Nation.

"PANTHER CAÑON WAS LIKE A thousand others—one of those abrupt fissures with which the earth in the Southwest is riddled; so abrupt that you might walk over the edge of any one of them on a dark night and never know what had happened to you.... The cañon walls, for the first two hundred feet below the surface, were perpendicular cliffs, striped with even-running strata of rock. From there on to the bottom the sides were less abrupt, were shelving, and lightly fringed with *piñons* and dwarf cedars.... At the very bottom of the cañon, along the stream, there was a thread of bright, flickering, golden-green—cottonwood seedlings."

Willa Cather, The Song of the Lark, *1915*

Canyon de Chelly by Raymond Jonson, 1928. *Phoenix Art Museum*
Opposite above: A storm brews over Monument Valley. *Photo David Harwood/Panoramic Images*
Opposite below: One of Arizona's "slot" canyons. *Photo Jerry Jacka*

Sunrise at Hopi Point, Grand Canyon, from a vantage point on the West Rim. The sun casts its first light over the endless panorama of the Canyon. Capturing this ever-changing spectacle is a challenge to painters and photographers alike. *Photo Warren Marr/Panoramic Images*

A mile deep and over 200 miles long, from 4 to 18 miles wide, the Grand Canyon of the Colorado is too vast, too complex, too overwhelming to comprehend in any simple way. As described by naturalist Joseph Wood Krutch, the Canyon is "the most revealing single page of earth's history anywhere open on the face of the globe"—a record of geologic time stretching back more than 1.5 billion years. Far down in the Inner Gorge can be seen black, twisted Archean rock, the oldest in the world. Piled up and up are strata deposited over eons —fossil-studded sandstone, shale, limestone—creating a rainbow-hued vision from afar.

The Canyon changes second by second as light plays over its mesas and spires. Clouds float over and through it. Winter brings snow to its forested rim, while deep within its walls there can be rain and pulsating heat. Far below, the Colorado races and tumbles over rock, as it has for all the millennia it has been creating this panorama. Artists and writers are frustrated by the quicksilver nature of the spectacle, yet irresistibly provoked to capture it. 🖎

"THE RHYTHM OF THE ROCKS BEATS VERY SLOWLY...THE MINUTE HAND OF ITS CLOCK moves by the millions of years.... And its second hand moves by the ceaseless

eroding drip of a seep spring, by the stinging flight of sand particles on a gray and windy evening, by the particle-on-particle accretion of white travertine in warm blue-green waters...."

Colin Fletcher,
The Man Who Walked Through Time, *1967*

Above: The Kaibab squirrel lives only on the high Kaibab Plateau on the Canyon's North Rim. The 9,000-foot-high plateau rims the Canyon at its deepest and widest point, across from the more heavily visited South Rim. As the Canyon widened, squirrel populations on either side became isolated. *Photo Tom and Pat Leeson/DRK Photo*

A Showery Day, Grand Canyon by Oscar E. Berninghaus, 1915. Around 1900, the railroad began to encourage tourism in the Grand Canyon; visitors flocked to stand before vistas like this one. *Burlington Northern Santa Fe Collection*

Encountering the Grand

The first humans to see the Grand Canyon—undoubtedly a band of prehistoric people wandering near its rim—left no record of their awed incomprehension. Nearly all who followed have done so, starting with the chronicler of Coronado's 1540 expedition. Human responses to the Canyon have run the gamut from terror to indifference to curiosity to reverence. Explorers and mystics, artists and entrepreneurs, tourists and scientists—all have been drawn to this most spectacular of places.

One remarkable early visitor came with an eye toward exploring the Canyon's wonders. In 1869, Major John Wesley Powell—one-armed Civil War veteran, Harvard-educated geologist and botanist—determined to run the entire length of the Colorado. With a nine-man crew, he set out in four flimsy boats to chart the hitherto unknown reaches of the Grand Canyon, thus becoming the first white man to make the complete trip. His success sparked an intense public fascination with the Canyon that has never abated.

"WE HAVE AN UNKNOWN DISTANCE YET TO RUN; an unknown river yet to explore. What falls there are, we know not; what rocks beset the channel, we know not; what walls rise over the river, we know not. Ah, well! we may conjecture many things.... With some eagerness, and some anxiety, and some misgiving, we enter the cañon below, and are carried along by the swift water through walls which rise from its very edge."

John Wesley Powell,
The Exploration of the Colorado River
of the West and Its Tributaries, *1875*

John Wesley Powell Speaking with Tai-Gu, Chief of the Paiutes. Photograph by John Hillers, 1872. Arizona Historical Society

Above: **An early tourist perches on the Canyon rim. Photograph by Fredrick L. King, 1914.** *Grand Canyon National Park*

The First Arizonans

Native American cultures have flourished for centuries in the land that is now Arizona. Experts and casual visitors alike marvel at the evidence left behind by the ancient ones—especially the ruins of their splendid buildings and fragments of distinctive pottery. By A.D. 1000, four

major civilizations were in full swing: the Anasazi, in the Colorado Plateau; the Hohokam of the lowland deserts; the mountain-country Mogollon; and the Sinagua of the Verde Valley. These people lived settled agricultural lives. The Hohokam developed a remarkable system of irrigation canals that enabled them to farm corn, beans, and squash. They also constructed "high-rises" of adobe; the arresting Casa Grande ruin testifies to their architectural skill. To the north, high in the walls of their canyon home, the Anasazi fashioned breathtaking stone cities, with multiple dwellings and large communal spaces called *kivas*. Mysteriously, these ancient people drifted away or simply vanished around A.D. 1300 to 1400. Yet later cultures, especially the Hopi, have kept alive the spirit and art of their ancient forebears. ❧

Blue sky and rainclouds in the distance
> we ride together
>> past cliffs with stories and songs
>> painted on rock.

>>> 700 years ago.

Paula Gunn Allen, from "Slim Man Canyon," 1972

Navajo Squaw Dance by Charlie Yazzie, 1965. The ritual dances of the Navajo are a central and enduring part of tribal life and faith. *National Museum of the American Indian. Below: Hosh-Cane-Ah-Sue-It, Navajo* by E. A. Burbank, c. early 1900s. Around the turn of the century, non-native artists grew fascinated with portraying Native American people and their traditional way of life. *Hubbell Trading Post National Historic Site*

Scholars believe that the Navajo—the Dineh—originally a nomadic people, arrived in the Four Corners area around A.D. 1350. Their culture merged with that of more settled peoples, and over time they turned to farming and raising sheep. Today the Navajo Nation, centered at Window Rock, stretches into New Mexico and Utah—the country's largest reservation, with the largest tribal population. Within its borders lies some of the Southwest's most spectacular scenery, all of it holy to the Navajo. The traditional Navajo way is based on achieving harmony with nature and one's fellow people. *Hozho,* or "walking in beauty," is the Dineh word for this harmony, and the concept extends into Navajo arts of all kinds. ✍

In beauty may I walk.

All day long may I walk.
Through the returning seasons may I walk.
On the trail marked with pollen may I walk.
With grasshoppers about my feet may I walk.
With dew about my feet may I walk.
With beauty may I walk.

From "The Mountain Chant"

Weaving Traditions

Arizona's Native American artisans are especially known for creating exceptional basketry and textiles. Basketry reaches the level of fine art among the Apache, the Hopi, and the Tohono O'odham (or Papago). The Hopi are also adept weavers, though the Navajo are most acclaimed for this traditional art. Older Navajo blankets were woven of subtly hued yarn dyed with vegetable colors; later, bright imported yarns were used. Both colors and designs were influenced by the Anglo newcomers; in fact trading posts encouraged the weaving of more salable rugs rather than blankets and serapes.

Above: Navajo silversmiths are noted for their beautiful concha belts; the domed silver conchas are embossed or stamped with designs. *The Heard Museum. Right:* Navajo Late Classic serape, c. 1870, woven of homespun yarns. *Morning Star Gallery, Santa Fe. Photo Addison Doty*

The Enduring Hopi

The Hopi of northern Arizona are the direct cultural descendants of the cliff-dwelling Anasazi and the Sinagua. Hopi life centers on a belief system called the *Hopivotskwani*—the Hopi Path of Life—an almost mystical union between humans and the natural world. Dwelling mostly on three high mesas in the heart of the surrounding Navajo Nation, they seem to live on an island, holding with stubborn faith to time-honored ways. The Hopi village of Oraibi is said to be the oldest continuously inhabited village in the United States, since A.D. 1150. While visitors are

allowed limited entry into the villages, the Hopi remain a very private people whose world outsiders experience mostly through their exquisite arts and crafts.

"SOTUKANG TOLD THE PEOPLE AS THEY stood at their Place of Emergence…'The name of this Fourth World is Tuwaqachi, World Complete…. It has height and depth, heat and cold, beauty and barrenness; it has everything for you to choose from…. Now you will separate and go different ways to claim all the earth for the Creator….Just keep your own doors open and always remember what I have told you.'"

Frank Waters, Book of the Hopi, 1963

Geronimo!

Like the Navajo, the Apache came to Arizona around A.D. 1300, but, unlike them, clung to their nomadic ways. At one point there were 23 independent bands—including the San Carlos, Aravaipa, White Mountain, and Chiricahua. The proud Apache refused to accept the encroachment of the Spanish and Anglos on their lands. They fought fiercely on and off through the 18th and 19th centuries, climaxing in the bloody Apache Wars from 1871 to 1886. Among many Apache leaders who won renown in these conflicts, no one fascinates as much as Geronimo, the great Chiricahua chief. His exploits were the stuff of legends; he was captured by the U.S. Army repeatedly but always managed to escape. At last, in 1886, he became a permanent prisoner of war. His people, finally subdued, were confined to their reservation.

Opposite above: Hopi Women Watching the Dancers. **Photograph by Edward Curtis, 1906. Hopi women were distinguished by their unique "squash-blossom" hairstyles.** *Opposite below: Walpi, Arizona* **by Peter Moran, 1883. Youngest brother of painter Thomas Moran, Peter visited Arizona in 1883.** *Amon Carter Museum Above:* **Apache olla basket, c. early 1900s.** *Private collection. Photo Jerry Jacka. Left:* **Geronimo, whose real name was Goyahkla, in his youthful prime.** *Arizona Historical Society*

"IT IS MY LAND, MY HOME, MY father's land, to which I now ask to be allowed to return. I want to spend my last days there and be buried among those mountains. If this could be I might die in peace...."

Geronimo,
Geronimo's Story of His Life, *1906*

Tumacácori Mission by Henry Cheever Pratt, c. 1854. The old Spanish mission of San José de Tumacácori, built in 1822, stands near Tubac, Arizona's oldest non-Indian settlement. *Phoenix Art Museum* *Below:* Statue of Father Eusebio Kino by George Phippen, 1964. The "Padre on Horseback" established 22 missions. *Phippen Museum. Opposite above:* Roof detail of San Xavier del Bac. *Photo David Burckhalter Opposite below:* Survey map of Arizona, 1866. *Arizona State Capitol Museum*

Missions and Seekers

The first Spanish explorers to make the trek up from Mexico found Arizona a profound disappointment. In 1540, Francisco Vasquez de Coronado traveled up the Gila River as far as the Hopi mesas, seeking a legendary treasure; instead he found a huddle of Native villages and, incidentally, the Grand Canyon. By the century's end, the Spanish had abandoned hope of gold and glory. But missionaries followed the soldiers, and their legacy was to prove more lasting. It was a mixed blessing of cultural clashes and mutual enrichment, warfare and peaceable husbandry, shaping Arizona over two centuries.

Arizona's Territorial days began in 1848, when the U.S. acquired part of it as spoils of the Mexican War. Gold, railroads, and a spirit of adventure spurred Anglo settlers westward into the new territory. A series of important Army surveys of the Far West, as well as a short-lived gold rush, were also instrumental in opening the Southwest. Inevitably

In Prescott, as in other Western towns at the turn of the century, Monday was washday for hard-working housewives. But one group of energetic and educated ladies bucked the trend and formed the Monday Club—Arizona's first women's club—in defiance of that tradition. Their purpose was to bring culture and the arts to this hard-drinking mining and ranching town. In the rarified mountain air, on quiet streets removed from wild Whiskey Row, literature and art, theater and music flourished and found supporters.

Untitled by Kate Cory, c. 1910–40. Cory's model was Mrs. Genung, a ranch wife and Prescott neighbor. In 1913, Cory took part in the famous Armory Show in New York. She also exhibited with the Society of Independent Artists. *Sharlot Hall Museum Right: Yavapai Lands* by Claire Dooner Phillips, c. 1950. *Private collection*

friendly groups. The Cowboy Artists of America was founded at Sedona's Oak Creek Tavern in 1965, for mutual support and promotion. Painters Joe Beeler, George Phippen, Charlie Dye, and John Hampton vowed in their charter to "perpetuate the memory and culture of the Old West...." The so-called Tucson Seven, it seems, was started mostly for fun by Howard Terpning, Bob Kuhn, Harley Brown, Tom Hill, Don Crowley, Ken Riley, and Duane Bryers. ↷

Inspired by the work of two great artists of the West, Frederic Remington (1861–1909) and Charles M. Russell (1864–1926), today's Western art depicts classic scenes of a bygone era as well as Western landscapes. Sunsets, deserts, cowboys, and Indians are usual subjects, often portrayed in an idealized way. The artists' styles vary from Don Crowley's hyperrealism to more impressionistic plein-air landscapes by such painters as Sedona-based Curt Walters. Many Western artists are sociable types with a penchant for organizing into

Above: Sierra Sky Scenic Boots by William Wilhelmi, 1982. Wilhelmi-Holland Gallery, Corpus Christi, Texas. Right: Afternoon Shadows at Maricopa Point by Peter Adams, 1995. The Grand Canyon is a favorite subject of plein-air painter Adams. Private collection. Opposite above: Against the Sunset by Frederic Remington, 1906. "With me," the artist wrote, "cowboys are what gems and porcelains are to others." Gerald Peters Gallery. Opposite below: Fry Bread by Don Crowley, 1996. Courtesy the artist

Navajos respectfully called *naalyehe ya sidaho* ("person who sits for things of value"). Now a National Historic Site, the post looks much as it did in times past—a friendly jumble of housewares, shoes, canned goods, and, of course, thousands of dollars worth of incomparable Navajo rugs. Scarcely a tourist goes by without stopping in.

"THEIR REMOTE POSTS WERE OASES IN THE DESERT, LANDMARKS in an unmarked wilderness. They were bankers, doctors, interpreters, school teachers, art agents, representatives of an encroaching white civilization to the Indians, and champions of Indian tribes against an inimical government."

Frank Waters, Masked Gods: Navajo and Pueblo Ceremonialism, *1950*

Two Navajo Men by Charlie Willeto, c. 1960. *National Museum of American Art/Art Resource Left:* Pictorial rug by Geanita John. *Garland's Navajo Rugs, Sedona Opposite above: Untitled by* E. A. Burbank. The interior of the venerable Hubbell Trading Post, c. 1908. Patrons gather around a wood stove. *Hubbell Trading Post National Historic Site Opposite below:* Maricopa two-headed pottery effigy, probably by Mabel Sunn or Barbara Johnson, c. 1950s. *Private collection Photo Jerry Jacka*

Trading Post Traditions

Trading posts were a rare point of peaceable contact between Native Americans and Anglos in the Arizona Territory. Beginning in the 1870s, Indians brought in their handmade blankets, baskets, jewelry, wool, and hides to trade for cloth, tools, and food. The institution was built on trust, fairness, and give-and-take negotiation. In prerailroad days, goods were laboriously hauled in by mule and ox-driven wagons; the Indians brought their wares on foot or horseback. The granddaddy of them all—Hubbell Trading Post—was established at Ganado, on the Navajo Reservation, in 1876. Its founder, J. L. Hubbell, was a fair-minded man whom the

grazed into exhaustion by the 1890s, the romance of cowboy life was firmly established, and ranch owners got rich. Both cattle and sheep ranchers competed for the same range. Today, much of the state is still dominated by ranches, including sheep raised by the Navajo in the Monument Valley area. Arizona is also cotton country. First practiced by ancient Native Americans, cotton farming became big business thanks to the extra-fine pima cotton developed here in the early 20th century. During the Depression, migratory workers flocked to the fields looking for work. Most cotton is grown in the irrigated Salt River Valley, where a long growing season makes possible three crops a year.

Migratory Cotton Picker, Eloy, Arizona. Photograph by Dorothea Lange, 1940. Lange's photos of destitute Dust Bowl refugees spoke volumes about their plight in the cotton fields of Arizona and other Western states. *International Museum of Photography at George Eastman House.* Left: Bleached cow skull. *Photo Jerry Jacka*

"'OH, JENNIE, WE ARE JUST A FEW days on the trail and I long for a meal at your table, with white cloths and glasses that shine! The chuck is beans, beef, and sourdough in endless combinations. Even pie is made with beans! And the cookie is a mean old man when he's crossed…'"

A homesick cowpuncher to his sweetheart,
in Cowboy: An Album *by*
Linda Granfield, 1994

Come all you jolly cowboys that follow the bronco steer,

I'll sing to you a verse or two your spirits for to cheer....

From the cowboy song "The Crooked Trail to Holbrook"

A Mix-Up by Charles M. Russell, 1910. Contrary to the romantic picture, the life of a working cowboy was a hard one. *Rockwell Museum, Corning, New York*

Cotton, Cattle, and Cowpokes

Cattle and sheep ranching, introduced by the Spanish, remain integral to Arizona's economy. In the days of the *ranchos*, cattle were herded by *vaqueros*, the original models for the Western cowboy. A cattle industry burgeoned in the high desert grasslands during Territorial days; while these fragile lands were

Copper by Philip Latimer Dike, 1935–36. Copper mining continues to be big business in Arizona up to the present day. *Phoenix Art Museum*

Below: A Navajo *ketoh*, or bow guard, of silver and leather, c. late 1800s. Silver mining produced a short-lived boom in Arizona. Much Navajo silver jewelry was made from Spanish silver coins and other imported material. *Arizona State Museum, University of Arizona*

"The earth was turned inside out….

Enterprising men hurried to the spot with barrels of whiskey and billiard tables;…traders crowded in with wagonloads of pork and beans; and gamblers came with cards and monte tables. There was everything in Gila City within a few months but a church and a jail, which were accounted barbarisms by the mass of the population."

A traveler on the short-lived town of Gila City, in Odie B. Faulk's Arizona: A Short History, *1970*

the newcomers clashed with Native Americans—especially the liberty-loving Apache—and, if less violently, with the Mexicans, by then comfortably established on their *ranchos.* The Anglo settlers who stayed established ranches, farms, mining operations, and the towns to support them.

"IT [SAN XAVIER] IS, WITHOUT QUIBBLE, the most beautiful man-made object in America Deserta....[T]he absolute, spectral whiteness—the most absolute whiteness that man-made pigment can achieve...prints on the retina of memory an image that will not go away."

Reyner Banham, Scenes in America Deserta, *1982*

"The White Dove of the Desert"

The magnificent church of San Xavier del Bac, near Tucson, appears like a shimmering mirage in the desert. The original mission on this site was destroyed in the Pima Rebellion in 1751. The present edifice, completed in 1797, is a breathtaking example of Spanish Baroque architecture. Its adobe walls, sheathed in white plaster, shine from afar; its portal is elaborately sculpted in a dizzying array of motifs. The equally fabulous interior features an intricately carved Baroque retablo and many frescoes.

U.S. Marshall Wyatt Earp of Tombstone, 1886. Photographer unknown. Earp became a legend even in his own time. After the famous 1881 shootout, he told his story to Stuart Lake, whose book *Wyatt Earp: Frontier Marshall* immortalized the man. *Western History Collections, University of Oklahoma Libraries Right:* Now a tourist attraction, Boot Hill cemetery was the prototypical Wild West graveyard. *Photo Superstock*

A prospector named Ed Schieffelin struck out into the hostile Arizona hills in 1877. He was told he'd find nothing but his tombstone; instead he made the biggest silver strike in Arizona history and founded a town. In the 1880s Tombstone was the quintessential "wild west"—a mining town legendary for violence and loose living. It had a newspaper called, ominously, the *Epitaph,* and a string of brothels and saloons that put the Barbary Coast to shame. Its most notorious shootout—the Earps versus the Clantons (none were "good guys")—was immortalized in the 1957 Western *Gunfight at the O.K. Corral.* Yet the "town too tough to die" had another side. Swollen with mining wealth, it was in its heyday larger than early San Francisco; citizens pointed with pride to their fine restaurants, serious theater, churches, and schools. Symbolic of this split personality was Allen Street: on one side were stores, cafés, and banks, while the other side roared with gaming houses and bordellos stocked with "fallen women." ❧

HERE
LIES

LESTER MOORE
FOUR SLUGS
FROM A-44
NO LES
NO MORE

Kirk Douglas and Burt Lancaster starred in the wildly popular 1957 movie *Gunfight at the O.K. Corral,* a romanticized retelling of the story behind the famed 1881 shootout. *Shooting Star. Below: Portrait of Frank Riley* by William Herbert Dunton, 1913. Riley was a lawman in Pima County in the 1880s. *Arizona Historical Society*

"KEEPING THEIR ALIGNMENT, ALMOST SHOULDER TO SHOULDER, the Earps and Holliday came on with lethal momentum. As they drew near, they pulled their guns. Holding their weapons at a level before them, they halted within five feet of the Clantons and McLowerys, so close that…they could look into the pupils of one another's eyes. The whisper of an Earp would have been audible to a Clanton.

'You fellows have been looking for a fight,' said Wyatt Earp, 'and now you can have it.'…

What happened now in the smoke of flaring guns happened while the clock ticked twenty seconds—twenty seconds packed with murderous hatred and flaming death."

The O.K. Corral showdown, from
Tombstone: An Iliad of the Southwest, *by Walter Noble Burns, 1929*

Boomtown Bonanza

Silver built Arizona's boomtowns of the 1870s—towns that sprang up almost overnight and were infamous for wild living, gambling, and violence. But it was copper that created lasting wealth. Financed by corporations back east, copper mining was practiced on a large scale. By around 1900, the towns of Bisbee, Jerome, Globe, and Clifton had become "company towns." People who made money from mining built handsome homes in the Victorian style; those that were preserved lend charm to their towns today. But copper mining was a nasty business for toilers in the pits; many died from accidents and disease, and all were under the thumb of the companies until the unions took a hand around 1917. Today, Arizona is still the nation's leading producer of copper, and its second nickname is the Copper State.

Among the members of the Monday Club were five serious artists, the so-called Five Ladies of Prescott. Claire Dooner Phillips, Kate T. Cory, Mabel Lloyd Lawrence, Ada Eldred Rigden, and Lillian Wilhelm Smith were all educated women and trained painters. Claire Dooner Phillips, who attended Stanford and Columbia Universities, was already an accomplished painter when she moved to Arizona in 1922; she later taught herself to make etchings. Ada Rigden, a teacher, studied painting with Claire Phillips in Prescott during the

Yaqui Indian Woman by Lucy Drake Marlow, 1928. While not considered one of the "Five Ladies," Marlow was among Arizona's first professional women artists, at home with oils, pastels, and charcoal. She settled in Tucson in 1927. *Lucy Drake Marlow Art Collection Trust*

1920s. Kate Cory, trained as a painter in New York, came West to photograph the Hopi tribes. She settled in Prescott in 1912; her landscape paintings are evocative and original views of Arizona's desert country. Prescott has inherited a legacy of museums from this era of women's art, including the Clara Dooner Phillips Memorial Fine Arts Center at Prescott College, funded by the estate of the artist (Clara was her given name) and her husband. ❧

Below: Desert Garden at the Buttes Mountaintop Resort in Tempe. *Photo Tom Bean. Opposite top:* Sun City Tucson, created by Del Webb, was the prototypical "adult community," attracting retirees with a carefully calibrated mix of homes, golf courses, pools, tennis courts, and other amenities. *Photo Mark Segal/Panoramic Images Opposite below: Dunlap Avenue Tree Guards— Man and Woman by Garth Edwards, 1990. Phoenix Arts Commission Photo Craig Smith*

In the years after World War II, Arizona sprinted forward and never looked back. Efficient air conditioning made the desert comfortable for people and industry. The promise of permanent sun, clean air, and new jobs lured retirees as well as young, ambitious workers, glad to escape from crowded Eastern cities and Midwestern winters. The state's population tripled between 1940 and 1970, then doubled again; by 1995 it had surpassed 4 million. Led by Motorola, industry and business migrated here starting in the 1950s; high-tech companies have lately followed suit. Today most Arizonans

live in cities like Phoenix, Tucson, and Flagstaff. Phoenix, in its youthful prime, gleams with steel and glass high-rises and sprawls into mile after mile of suburbs. Its booming energy drives a growing civic pride that includes support of the arts. Smaller Tucson prides itself on its cultural sophistication and

distinctive character; Tusconans sometimes worry
about getting "too big." Of course, tourism accounts
for a huge share of Arizona's prosperity. Countless
resorts cater to vacationers. And in planned communities that feel like resorts (Del Webb's Sun City
Tucson is the prototype), retirees enjoy golf, swimming, and tennis just steps from their doors. ✎

> "ROOM TO BREATHE—COUNTRY LIVING
> MINUTES FROM PHOENIX—ONE-ACRE
> MINI-RANCHES—HORSE PRIVILEGES AND
> BRIDLE PATH"
>
> *Sign advertising a development near Phoenix*

At the center of the sky, the holy boy walks four ways with life.

Just mine, my mountain became; standing toward me with life.
The dancers became; standing toward me with life.

White Mountain Apache

Fertility Symbols by **Waldo Mootzka (Hopi), c. 1930s.** *Gilcrease Museum, Tulsa* **Right: Hopi kachina dolls (c. 1900) represent Si'ohemiskatsina and Nimankatsina and figure in the Niman ceremony, held after the summer solstice. Their headpieces symbolize clouds and rain.** *The Heard Museum*

For Arizona's Native peoples, religion is bound to the rhythms of nature and woven into every part of life—art and craft, work and community. Arts such as sandpainting, pottery and basket decoration, and textiles always contain spiritual symbolism, often in the form of motifs from nature—zigzag lightning, spiral forms, stars. Much art has a spiritual purpose; sandpainting is a healing ritual, for example. Faith is also expressed in ritual dance.

While they may seem merely a colorful spectacle to outsiders, these dances are actually a profound meeting of the human and spiritual worlds. Beautiful objects like the Hopi kachina figures and masks and the Apache *ga'an* masks are made in connection with ritual dances, and spectacular body paint often plays a role. ❧

Sacred Rituals

A powerful Hopi ritual is the 16-day Snake–Antelope Ceremony, which invokes the spirit of the rain. In the dramatic Snake Dance, men dance while holding rattlers or other snakes in their mouths. In Frank Waters's classic *Book of the Hopi,* Koahwyma, a member of the Hopi Snake Society, describes the night of blessing and entertaining the snakes deep in the kiva, before the Snake Dance is held: "There were all kinds of snakes: rattlesnakes, big bull snakes, racers, sidewinders, gopher snakes—about sixty all tangled on the floor. The singing stirred them. They moved in one direction, then another, looking over all the men in the circle. The men never moved. They just kept singing with a kind expression on their faces....Then a big yellow rattler moved slowly toward an old man singing with eyes closed, climbed up his crossed leg, coiled in front of his breechcloth and went to sleep....That is the way snakes show who are good and kind men with pure hearts...."

Hopi Snake Dance, Number I by Jan Matulka, 1917–18. *Whitney Museum of American Art. Photo Geoffrey Clements*

Saints and Small Miracles

Roman Catholicism came to Arizona with the Spanish missionaries, and it has been a powerful force in shaping life here ever since. Much architecture, art, and craft work, especially that of Hispanic artists, has its roots in religious expression. Missions and churches like San José de Tumacácori and San Xavier del Bac express the community's faith on a grand scale. But devotion is also shown in smaller, personal ways. In San Xavier del Bac, as in other Arizona churches, worshippers bedeck statues with hundreds of *milagros*—little cast-metal (sometimes gold or silver) figures of men, women, and children, body parts, cows, even cars. *Milagros* ("miracles" in Spanish) are offered to the saints in supplication or as thanks for curing disease or misfortune. And in the front yards of Hispanic homes, people often create *nichos,* small shrines to favorite saints. In some places the blending of Native American and Catholic traditions has produced unique folkways and religious folk art, as in the Tohono O'odham *nacimientos*—handmade crèche scenes with homely everyday details.

Santo by Raymond Jonson, 1929. Santos—little statues of saints—are folk-art figures traditionally carved of wood and painted. *Roswell Museum and Art Center*

"Oh, yes, we were the best Catholics.
We walked from Ajo to Gila Bend to Yuma
    and places in between.
We walked to Quitobaquito there at Organ Point
    and on down to Rocky Point.
And all the while we carried an extra suitcase
    just for the saints."…
My mother, she didn't know. She had so many
    saints and bottles of holy water.
She carried them, sometimes on horseback,
    but mostly on foot.
Every evening, wherever we stopped, she opened her suitcase
and set the saints out

Ofelia Zepeda, from "Suitcase of Saints," 1995

Above: The time-honored ritual of attaching *milagros* to statues of the saints is practiced by Indians and Mexican Americans alike. *Photo courtesy El Potrero Trading Post*
Left: Detail of *Nacimiento* by Maria Luisa Teña, c. 1978–present. This charming scene is part of a large, ever-evolving exhibit by the artist at the Tucson Museum's La Casa Cordova. *Photo Edward McCain*

"I HAD LIVED AND WORKED IN THE WEST AND KNEW what irrigation meant to the West. I knew the utter impossibility of expecting the larger schemes to be developed by private enterprise…and was, therefore, already anxious to have…this piece of work done by the only individual that could do it, Uncle Sam."

President Theodore Roosevelt, at the dedication of the Roosevelt Dam, 1911

Damming the Canyons

Water: in a mostly desert land, people pray for it, fight over it, use all their ingenuity to get it. Ancient Native Americans, the Hohokam, dug a system of ditches to carry precious water to their fields; when their remnants were discovered some 800 years later, they formed the basis for a new irrigation system that ultimately gave rise to modern-day Phoenix. Until the late 19th

century, ditches and canals were still the only form of irrigation. Around 1900 began the era of mammoth public projects, built with federal funds for fast-growing populations. Arizona's first major water project was the mighty Roosevelt Dam, completed in 1911 as the first step in the Salt River Project. A later series of dams along the Salt and Verde Rivers provided hydroelectric power and created huge lakes and reservoirs. The result: a "greenbelt" of irrigated land that

made possible the urban Arizona of today. Also within Arizona lie the Hoover Dam and the controversial Glen Canyon Dam, completed in 1963. These great works of engineering have their own grandeur—yet they draw fire from environmentalists and some Natives, who object that dams forever alter natural river ecologies and may encroach on land and water rights. ⟩

Lake Powell 2 by Diane Burko, 1980. This vast lake was created when Glen Canyon Dam was built. *Marion Locks Gallery, Philadelphia* Opposite above: Teddy Roosevelt at the dedication of his namesake dam. *The Heard Museum* Opposite below: Bridge over Lake Powell and Glen Canyon. *Photo Ric Erginbright/Corbis*

"SHOULD WE ALSO FLOOD THE SISTINE CHAPEL so tourists can get closer to the ceiling?"

David Brower, in a Sierra Club public service ad protesting a mid-1960s plan to dam part of the Colorado just above Grand Canyon. Brower and the Club still mourn the drowning of Glen Canyon by the dam there.

The home and studio at Taliesin West, now the quarters of the Frank Lloyd Wright School of Architecture, are among Wright's most admired works. *Photo Julius Shulman. Below:* The dramatic Chapel of the Holy Cross, designed by Marguerite Brunswig Staude and built in 1956, is an inspiring sight rising above Sedona's famed red cliffs. *Photo L. Mulvehill/ Image Works*

Desert Visionaries

The desert's stark beauty—its colors, forms, and planes— provides timeless inspiration for architects, from the earliest builders in adobe and stone to contemporary practitioners.

The latter, especially Frank Lloyd Wright, sometimes took their cue from the organic forms created by ancient predecessors. Already an eminent architect when he began visiting Arizona in the 1920s, Wright found in the desert a revelation and a test. In 1937 he began work on the twin to his famous Taliesin in Wisconsin—Taliesin West, near Scottsdale. In all, Wright designed about 50 buildings for Arizona (not all of them built), including private

homes, the First Christian Church in Phoenix, and the ornate Gammage Center on the University of Arizona campus. An earlier architect took her cue directly from the ancient Native builders: Mary Colter designed notable hotel buildings and interiors for the Fred Harvey Company. Italian architect and visionary Paolo Soleri also found wide-open Arizona (near Prescott) the perfect setting for his work. He is in the process of creating Arcosanti, a small-scale prototype of his vision for a self-contained city. Set amid the desert rocks, this glass, concrete, and steel complex is a striking sight.

Left: Paolo Soleri's bronze bells at Arcosanti, a live-and-work community driven by the architect's vision of the future. At Soleri's retreat, notes one writer, "two classic coolants of the fevered brow—tinkling bells and tinkling fountains—delight the ear." *Below:* Mary Colter's Watch-tower, on the South Rim of the Grand Canyon. Colter's respect for the ancient builders is seen here and in her other buildings at the Canyon. *Photos Jack Parsons*

"OUT HERE IN THE GREAT SPACES OBVIOUS symmetry would claim too much, I find, the too obvious wearies the eye too soon, stulti-fies imagination....[The] Arizona character seems to cry out for a space-loving architec-ture of its own. The straight line and flat plane, sun-lit, must come here—of all places—but they should become the dotted line, the broad, low, extended plane textured because in all this astounding desert there is not one hard undotted line to be seen."

Frank Lloyd Wright, An Autobiography, *1932*

The best-preserved stretch of old Route 66 lies in Arizona, between Seligman and Toprock. *Right:* Route 66 mural, on the historic Beale Hotel in Kingman, depicts a 1940s-era bus driver. *Below:* Neon beacon in Kingman. *Photos Vincent J. Musi Opposite above:* Untitled mural by Maynard Dixon, c. 1907, commissioned for the Tucson Depot of the Southern Pacific Railroad. *Private collection. Photo Arizona Historical Society Opposite below:* Our Human Roots, Nuestras Raices Humanas *by Antonio Pazos (left side) and David Tineo (right side), 1985. Tucson Art Museum Photo Chuck Place*

Camels to Cars: On Route 66

The thoroughfare that became the fabled Route 66 was busy and colorful even in Arizona's early days. In 1857, Lieutenant Edward F. "Ned" Beale, surveying the 35th parallel, used camels for pack animals. His caravan, driven by imported Arab, Greek, and Turkish drivers in traditional robes, must have been quite a sight. Modern-day Route 66—variously called the Mother Road and America's Main Street—was officially designated in 1927. For decades after, until the sad day in 1984 when the interstate replaced it, the road was an avenue of legends. Dust-bowl migrants and soldiers, fortune seekers and tourists—everyone traveled "out west" on Route 66. The eccentric motels, cafés, trading posts, gas stations, and billboards that sprouted along the length of the grand old road only enhanced its tawdry glamour.

In the Public Eye

Beginning in the late 1960s, mural art began to appear on buildings in urban Arizona, especially in the Hispanic community of South Tucson. Outdoor art is well adapted to the Sun Belt, where the inspiration of the great Mexican muralists also is close at hand. Some murals advertise goods and services on the sides of buildings, or in one case on a taco van decorated with ranch cooking scenes. Others are created as paeans to cultural identity—or to forestall the invasion of graffiti. Many murals by Hispanic artists, such as Luis Mena, combine traditional and contemporary imagery—auto tires and Aztec gods, for example.

Right: Metalwork lizard detail on an adobe building in Tucson, craftsman unknown. *Photo Jack Parsons*
Below: Jay Hawkinson garden by landscape architect Steve Martino. This garden in Phoenix takes inspiration from desert cultures, old and new. Its colorful sculptures and walls pay homage to the noted Mexican landscape designer Luis Barragán. *Photo John Samora*

Native American, Hispanic, and Anglo "Old West" traditions mingle with new trends to create a wide range of Arizona lifestyles. Homes and gardens, decorative arts, and especially cooking all display a bold creativity in combining traditional and contemporary themes. The classic Spanish adobe homes, along with age-old Spanish crafts like wrought-iron work and furniture-making, are much respected yet freely adapted to suit today's residents. The Old West survives,

too, on sprawling cattle ranches and in small towns like Bisbee and Prescott, where many dwellings were built with mining wealth. In some places, life is unabashedly 20th-century: Phoenix and Tucson feature the high-rise downtowns, parks, malls, and urban sprawl common to most American cities.

The Empie residence in Carefree, known as the Boulder House, was designed by Charles Johnson in 1986. *Photo Jack Parsons. Below:* The Steinfeld Mansion in Tucson, a classic example of the Mission Revival style. *Photo Edward McCain*

And the sun-drenched leisure lifestyle of retirement communities, native to the Sun Belt, is founded on air conditioning, golf courses, Eastern-style lawns, and swimming pools—amenities hard on the desert environment. But there's a movement toward homes that hark back to traditional styles and materials, such as naturally insulating adobe, and to landscaping that celebrates the hardy natives in place of water-hungry exotics. ƍ

Desert Dwellings

Arizona homes are as varied as their inhabitants, from the earth-made Navajo hogan to a condo high-rise. A tour of Arizona homes is a stroll through history, beginning with the shelters carved by the ancients into lofty canyon walls. Adobe pueblos, Navajo hogans, and Apache wickiups follow. Next are the Spanish adobes: one-room houses or *ranchos* with graceful verandas. With the advent of Anglos, adobe dwellings were overlain with Eastern building styles or replaced entirely by ornate gingerbread Victorians, complete with flower beds. In contemporary times, major architectural revivals—notably the Mission Revival and Spanish Colonial

Revival styles—pay homage to older models. In another kind of harkening back, homes designed by Frank Lloyd Wright and others draw from the forms and substance of the land itself. Today's cutting-edge designs, such as those of Antoine Predock, carry this concept still further. Materials like adobe, sandstone, and even rammed earth compose the structures; and instead of green lawns with cottage-garden borders, the new landscapes feature native cactus and ocotillo, mesquite and paloverde.

"AQUÍ ESTABA MI CASITA. IT WAS MY FATHER'S HOUSE. And his father's house before that. They built it with their own hands with adobes made from the mud of the river. When it rained, the adobes smelled like the good clean earth....See here! I had a fig tree growing. In the summer I gave figs to the neighbors and birds...."

Patricia Preciado Martin, "The Journey," 1980

Opposite above: A Tucson residence, built in 1992. *Photo David Fox*
Opposite below: The 1895 Victorian Rosson House is now a museum. *Photo Richard Cummins/Corbis*
Above: Handpainted wooden chair by Patrick Murillo and Kathy Cano-Murillo of Los Mestizos, 1996. *Photo John Samora. Left:* The interior of artist Anne Coe's home features local artisanwork: a banquette with longhorn embossing and a lamp with a cholla cactus base. *Photo Jack Parsons*

Celebrating the Circle of Life

Arizona's Hispanic folk arts spring from time-honored community rituals and celebrations, and have been adopted by Arizonans of all backgrounds. Colorful paper craftwork is a tradition from Mexico. Families decorate graves and church altars with elaborate tissue paper flowers—especially on All Souls Day—and similar flowers brighten weddings and fiestas. No child's birthday party would be complete without a *piñata* to break. These fringed papier-mâché figures take every conceivable form, from animals to space invaders; they also figure in the Christmastime Los Posadas celebration. A less familiar tradition are *cascarones:* eggshells are hollowed out, filled with confetti, and decorated, then broken over the celebrants' heads at Easter and various fiestas. Working in wrought iron is yet another art imported from Mexico.

In the old days, hand-wrought fences, window gratings, and tools served both practical and aesthetic purposes. Other objects were made purely for their beauty and meaning: church details, for example, or crosses at gravesites.

Traditional Mexican piñatas are made of pottery instead of papier-mâché; they are usually filled with candies and small toys that shower on the lucky child who manages to break them with a stick. *Photo Linda Husted* *Right:* **This Día de los Muertos altar by Mesa artist Virginia Aguero is decorated with traditional paper flowers.** *Arizona Historical Society Photo Chuck Place*

No quiero oro, ni quiero plata,
Lo que yo quiero es quebrar la piñata.

(I don't want gold and I don't want silver.
All I want is to break the piñata.)

"Canción de Piñata," a child's song

"WHEN I WAS A YOUNG GIRL WE WOULD go to the Placita.…There was a gazebo in the center of the plaza and a string orchestra played there.…We would sit on the boulders or on the grass and listen.…We would be all dressed up with long beautiful dresses and we wore hats with feathers or flowers. Everything was handmade in those days.… My mother was a beautiful seamstress. We even made our own hats."

Elina Laos Sayre, in Images and Conversations: Mexican-Americans Recall a Southwestern Past *by Patricia Preciado Martin, 1983*

Spanish wrought-iron gate, c. 18th or 19th century. *Oakland Museum of California. Above:* Tinwork candle holder for Día de los Muertos (Day of the Dead). *Photo Chuck Place*

A saguaro harvest, illustration from *Desert Giant* by Barbara Bash. The Tohono O'odham people harvest saguaro cactus fruit to make jam, syrup, and wine. *Courtesy Sierra Club Books* *Below:* Label for Arizona Gunslinger jalapeño pepper sauce. *Arizona Pepper Products Co.*

Creative cooks have ransacked Arizona's cupboard of cultural flavors to create an irresistible cuisine. Native ingredients, traditional Mexican dishes, and chuck-wagon chow are the basic ingredients, all making use of key staples such as beans, corn, and chiles. Both Native American and Mexican cooks add fiery chiles to enliven soups and stews, tacos and burritos, and the state's signature dish, the *chimichanga*—a big flour tortilla wrapped around beef or chicken, beans, and chiles, then deep-fried. Beans are eaten everywhere. Dished out from the "cookie's" iron pot along with beef and biscuits, beans mean home on the range for the hungry wrangler. At the opposite end of the

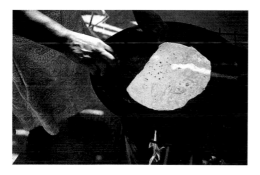

Desert Salsa

1 cup cholla buds (rehydrated, cooked, cooled)
1 cup cooked or canned nopalitos
½ medium onion
1 clove garlic
2 tomatoes
½ cup chuparosa flowers
1 tbsp. salt
2 tbsp. minced oregano
Juice of ½ lemon or lime

Chop first 6 ingredients and mix with seasonings. Serve with corn chips. (To prepare cholla and nopalitos: rinse dried buds, cover with boiling water, soak at least 30 minutes. Add water if needed; simmer until tender. Cool and scrape remaining spines.)

spectrum, chefs in upscale restaurants craft menus using hearty, indigenous elements and techniques from far and wide. Some have incorporated (via the Native Americans) wild edible plants such as saguaro fruit, cholla buds, prickly-pear *(nopales)*, baby tumbleweed, and purslane, or *verdolagas*, a spinachlike weed—as well as heirloom or "antique" beans. Other flavors in the Arizona pantry are local crop foods such as grapefruit, blue corn, dates, and figs. ❧

Above: **Tortilla making at a Tohono O'odham saguaro harvest camp.** *Photo Stephen Trimble/ DRK Photo. Right:* **A plate of tamales steamed in corn husks, a traditional holiday dish of Mexican and Indian heritage.** *Photo Edward McCain*

At the old ball game in Tucson, fans soak up the sun. Teams also play in stadiums in Peoria, Scottsdale, Phoenix, Tempe, Mesa, and Chandler. Spring Training in Arizona got started when Cleveland Indians owner Bill Veeck organized practice near his winter home in Tucson. *Photo Mike Scully/ Adstock. Opposite above:* The sandstone faces of Monument Valley make a dramatic backdrop for hot air balloons. *Photo Dewitt Jones/Tony Stone Images. Opposite below:* Outdoor sports like kayaking are a natural in Arizona, where breathtaking settings seem to inspire heart-stopping athletic feats among hardier souls. *Photo Joel Rogers/Corbis*

Leisure is pursued with passion in Arizona, where outdoor recreation is a year-round proposition. Arizonans love to hike and camp, and, in winter, ski or snowshoe in the mountains. Riders and rockhounds, cyclists and amateur gold panners brave the Southwest sun in droves. Hot-rodding and low-riding head the list of car hobbies. Surprisingly, water sports flourish in this desert state: the Colorado and lesser rivers draw adventurers from far and wide for world-class whitewater rafting and kayaking. Less daring types cast for trout in wild rivers and streams. The reservoirs created by Arizona's huge dams—Lakes Powell, Mead, and Havasu—are

places to swim, water-ski, or just putter around on a rented houseboat.

Spectator sports are big, too. The NFL's Phoenix Cardinals, the NBA Phoenix Suns, and hockey's Phoenix Roadrunners play in Arizona. Major golf tournaments are held on spectacular courses. But the most beloved local sporting tradition is Cactus League Baseball, better known as Spring Training. Eight or so teams call the state home from February to April; they include the San Francisco Giants, Seattle Mariners, Chicago Cubs, and Colorado Rockies. Fans from around the country follow, for the late-winter sunshine and the old-time sandlot atmosphere. ☞

> *"There was never a horse that couldn't be rode,*
> *and there was never a cowboy that couldn't be thrown."*
>
> Old rodeo saying

Of Greens and Greenhorns

Raging Bull by Michael Marsh, 1997. Rodeos have long been popular entertainment all over Arizona; Prescott is home to the Frontier Days event, one of the world's oldest professional rodeos. *Suzanne Brown Gallery, Scottsdale*

Arizona is golf heaven; it boasts more than 225 courses, many created by famous designers such as Robert Trent Jones and players Arnold Palmer and Jack Nicklaus. Year-round sun and warmth lure amateurs and professionals alike, especially to big events like the Phoenix Open. Visitors seeking more a rough-and-ready experience come to Arizona's famous dude ranches. Dude ranching was born in the 1920s around Wickenburg, which still bills itself as the "Dude Ranch Capital of the

72   PASTIMES

World." These resorts, some of them well-preserved period pieces, offer "city slickers" a chance to ride the range, eat chuck-wagon chow, and breathe dust like real cowhands. And what would a Western experience be without a rodeo? Arizona hosts countless amateur, junior, and professional events featuring barrel riding, calf roping, saddle broncs, Brahma bulls, and clowns. All make for exciting and unpredictable entertainment.

"ALL THIS WINTER WE MIGHT HAVE BEEN A FAMILY OF TARTARS. The oldest pair of children have spent their days in colored shirts and scarves, blue jeans and sombreros, riding, practicing for local rodeos, and talking about riding and rodeos;... when they were not riding cow ponies, they turned themselves into ponies, galloping about on all fours...."

J. B. Priestly, Midnight on the Desert, *1937*

Lawn bowling at Sun City. *Photo Mike Yamashita/Corbis.* **Below: Hole 16 at the pinnacle course, Troon North Golf Club, Scottsdale.** *Photo Henebry Photography*

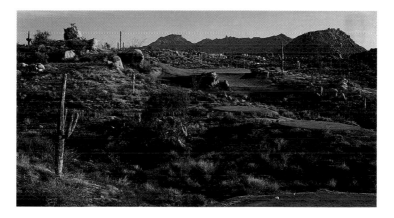

Black Sheep, Strobridge Lithograph Co., 1894. American playwright Charles Hoyt, inventor of the comedy-farce, based this play on his experiences as a cowboy and set it in Tombstone, Arizona. *Library of Congress Poster Collection Below:* In the 1994 film *Geronimo,* Cherokee actor Wes Studi played the great Apache chief. *Shooting Star*

On Stage and Screen

For moviegoers from Paris to Tokyo, the enduring image of the American West features cowboys or cavalry or Indian riders racing hell-for-leather across a dusty desert. Almost invariably, those scenes were shot against the rock towers and red dirt of Arizona's Monument Valley. It was director John Ford who made this landscape so universally known, in classic films such as *Stagecoach* (starring John Wayne, of course), *The Searchers*, *Fort Apache*, and *Rio Grande*. Arizona lore inspired another famous "oater," *Gunfight at the O.K. Corral* (1957), a romanticized version of the famous Tombstone shootout. Sedona, with its dramatic red rocks, was also a popular locale for filming. And Old Tucson Studios, built for the 1939 Western *Arizona*, has been used over the years for countless movies and TV shows; it's still a working studio as well as a tourist attraction. On the stage, Arizona's vision of itself (and the world) widens considerably. The state is justly proud of its highly acclaimed Arizona Theatre Company, founded in Tucson in 1967. The drama season is divided between there and Phoenix; the two cities also support smaller theater companies, including Spanish-language and Spanish–English theater.

"HUNDREDS OF NAVAJOS WERE cast as Apache, Cheyenne, Comanche, and other Indians, but they always spoke Navajo. Noted for their keen sense of humor, some of the lines would never have made it past a Navajo-speaking censor. When the film played theaters in Flagstaff and Winslow, whites were bewildered by…Navajos in the audience who snickered during some of the more serious dialogue.…"

Marshall Trimble, Roadside History of Arizona, *1986*

Left: In the 1920s and 30s, Tom Mix was *the* Western movie idol. With his beloved horse, Tony, he starred in dozens of B-movie Westerns, combining stunts and horsemanship with shoot-'em-up action. *Photo Library of Congress. Above:* Poster by Michele Wood for the Arizona Theater Company's production of Athol Fugard's *Valley Song*, 1997–98 season. *Arizona Theater Company*

Tales of the West

In the many forms of Arizona's literature, the Western myth is celebrated, mourned, scrutinized, satirized, or turned on its head. The traditional songs of the Navajo, Hopi, Papago, and Pima, as collected and translated by ethnologists, are some of the West's truest poetry. Contemporary Native voices such as Joy Harjo and Ramson Lomatewana invoke their ancestors through the weave of their own experience. Hispanic writers, like Patricia Preciado Martin, also

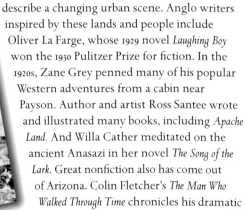

describe a changing urban scene. Anglo writers inspired by these lands and people include Oliver La Farge, whose 1929 novel *Laughing Boy* won the 1930 Pulitzer Prize for fiction. In the 1920s, Zane Grey penned many of his popular Western adventures from a cabin near Payson. Author and artist Ross Santee wrote and illustrated many books, including *Apache Land.* And Willa Cather meditated on the ancient Anasazi in her novel *The Song of the Lark.* Great nonfiction also has come out of Arizona. Colin Fletcher's *The Man Who Walked Through Time* chronicles his dramatic

solo walk through the Grand Canyon; Frank Waters's classic studies have enhanced our knowledge of and respect for Hopi ways. Edward Abbey's *Cactus Country* is a landmark portrait of the Sonoran Desert. Popular genres—cowboy poetry, humor, and journalism—also flavor the literary scene.

Zane Grey by Soss Melik, 1939. Many of Grey's romantic and thrilling Western novels were set in Arizona. The wildly popular author built a hunting cabin in 1920 near Payson, where he visited on and off for nine years. Today it's a museum dedicated to his life and works. *National Portrait Gallery/ Art Resource.* Below: Cover illustration by J. W. Scott for the pulp novel *Keep Loading, Jenny,* c. 1930s–40s. *Meyer Gallery, Scottsdale*

"WHAT WAS IT THAT CONFOUNDED HER SIGHT? DESERT slope—down and down—color—distance—space! The wind that blew in her face seemed to have the openness of the whole world back of it. Cold, sweet, dry, exhilarating, it breathed of untainted vastness. Carley's memory pictures of the Adirondacks faded into pastorals; her vaunted images of European scenery changed to operetta settings. She had nothing with which to compare this illimitable space. 'Oh!—America!' was her unconscious tribute."

Zane Grey, The Call of the Canyon, *1921*

"IT'S TRUE THE LANDSCAPE FORMS THE MIND. IF I STAND here long enough I'll learn how to sing. None of that country & western heartbreak stuff, or operatic duets, but something cool as the blues, or close to the sound of a Navajo woman singing early in the morning."

Joy Harjo, Secrets from the Center of the World, *1989*

MUSICAL TRADITIONS

Diverse traditions play counterpoint in Arizona's music. Local folk music is enriched by Mexican harmonies and rhythms, Native chants, and cowboy ballads. The classic Mexican import is *mariachi:* in *charro* costumes bedecked with embroidery and silver, musicians on violin, trumpet, guitar, and the king-size *guitarron* enliven social events as well as street and concert performances. Also from Mexico comes the popular *folklorico* dance form. Arizona has bred some amazing hybrids, such as Papago "chicken scratch" music, also called *waila.* Played at a fast tempo, it usually

accompanies a six-beat dance step that some say looks like a chicken scratching the ground! Musically it's a wild blending of Eastern European polka and Mexican instruments. Another distinctive sound is *la música norteña,* featuring accordion, saxophone, guitar, fiddle, and drums. And Tejano, the hugely popular mingling of Latin and pop-rock sounds, has survived the untimely death of its star, Serena.

The European classics are well represented by the

Above: Now popular the world over, *folklorico* dancing is a stylized, spectacularly costumed version of traditional Mexican dancing. It's performed at many public festivals, especially around the Cinco de Mayo holiday. *Photo Richard Embery/Adstock. Above right:* A *ricinto,* a type of Spanish guitar. *Photo John Samora. Right:* Performers at Tucson's International Mariachi Festival. *Photo David Burckhalter*

venerable Tucson Symphony, the Phoenix Symphony, the Phoenix Opera, and many other orchestras and chamber groups. Composer Ferde Grofe's *Grand Canyon Suite,* with its rhythms of burro hoof-beats descending a canyon trail, evokes that landmark universally; it's even the background music for a canyon diorama at Disneyland. Throw in a shot of jazz, and Arizona lives a rich musical life indeed.

> It is 1:30 A.M.
> Sleep won't come.
> She listens to music.
> O'odham waila music. San Antonio Rose,
> a wild saxophone and accordion.
> In her mind she dances.
> She dances with a handsome cowboy....
> The earth dance floor beneath them,
> the stars and moon above them.
> That rhythm, that rhythm,
> it makes them one.
>
> *Ofelia Zepeda, from "Waila Music," 1995*

The Ronstadt Dynasty

Vocalist Linda Ronstadt, from an old Tucson family, was born to be musical. Her great-great-grandfather, Federico Ronstadt, arrived in 1882 from Sonora, Mexico, and founded the Club Filarmonico, one of Tucson's first orchestras. Linda's great-aunt, Luisa Ronstadt Espinel, sang opera and Spanish folk music on the international circuit. Ronstadt herself has recorded traditional Mexican *canciónes.*

Above left: Album cover of the *waila* group Gu-Achi Fiddlers. *Courtesy Canyon Records. Photo Robert Doyle. Above:* Luisa Ronstadt Espinel. *Arizona Historical Society*

Arizona Altar by George L. K. Morris, 1949. Morris was among just a few of Arizona's "visiting" artists to work in an abstract mode. This work uses fragments of a ceremonial mask and a kachina doll. *Hunter Museum of Art, Chattanooga*

Some places seem to attract an outsized share of artists, musicians, and other creative people. Arizona has several "arts towns"—Jerome, Tubac, and Prescott among them, but none more dramatic than Sedona. Set against a backdrop of sandstone buttes that blaze red in the sun, this town is a magnet for creative activity. Some say its magnetism is literal, arising from the convergence of no fewer than seven "vortices" that focus electromagnetic energy. Founded in 1902 by Missourians Carl and Sedona Schnebly, Sedona became an art colony in the 1960s and later a New Age mecca. Today it's a booming art center with an estimated 300 working artists and some 50 galleries. Among the notables to "discover" Sedona was the German-born surrealist painter Max Ernst (1891–1976). A more local group, the Cowboy Artists of America, was founded here in the 1960s. Sedona also draws musicians; the annual Jazz on the Rocks festival is a fixture. 🐦

"There I found the old familiar landscape

that had continually been in my mind's eye, and which had repeatedly appeared in my paintings, too."

Max Ernst, in a 1991 documentary film

Above: Colline Inspirée (Inspired Hill) by Max Ernst, 1950. Arriving in 1946 with his wife, painter Dorothea Tanning, Ernst felt he had found his artistic and spiritual home in Sedona. There they spent a seven-year idyll of painting, sculpting, and touring around.

The Menil Collection, Houston Right: Harmony in the Red Rocks by David Fischel, 1997. Every September Sedona hosts the world-famous Jazz on the Rocks festival, a sellout since its inception in 1982. This work became a festival poster. *Courtesy the artist*

Arizona's recent flowering of the arts encompasses every form, from painting and sculpture to weaving to photography. Part of the challenge for artists lies in capturing the essence of people and places that are both ancient and brand-new. Artists who have spent their lives here often look for new ways to express their relationship with place and with their traditional cultures. Navajo painters Grey Cohoe and Aaron Freeland put a contemporary spin on traditional forms and designs. Dan Namingha, and Linda

Lomahaftewa, of Hopi descent, use traditional iconography in more abstract styles of painting and sculpture. Others, coming to Arizona from outside, are spellbound by its light, space, and landforms, which they interpret in myriad ways. The canvases of Lynn Taber-Borcherdt explore the drama of desert skies and weather, while Merrill Mahaffey's large-scale paintings combine realism and abstraction to portray monumental forms. Still others explore personal rather than place-specific themes in Arizona's warmly receptive arts climate. ❧

> *"I have always used humor as a vehicle for my messages."*
>
> Anne Coe, *in* Leading the West *by Donald J. Hagerty, 1997*

Suburban Ranchette: Utopian Bliss at the End of the Millennium by Anne Coe, 1996. Coe enjoys juxtaposing dissonant images to make a point: here, a cowgirl and longhorn steer in suburbia. Joy Tash Gallery. Photo Bill McLemore

Primeval Meets Postmodern

While Arizona's natural environment has always compelled artists, now an emerging urban landscape offers itself for interpretation as well. How the old and the new clash or harmonize is a favorite theme; the paintings of Anne Coe, for example, combine nostalgic and modern elements in sometimes outrageous ways. Photographers, too, have long been drawn to record the drama of light and shadow, rock and sky; the University of Arizona's Center for Creative

Photography in Tucson boasts an outstanding photography collection and regularly shows work from around the world. Today's photographers, too, often explore the contrasts of "old" and "new" West. The documentary images of the late Louis Carlos Bernal illuminate religious and family ties in Arizona's Chicano community. Other art forms don't just portray the land but are part of it. Earthworks, such as James Turrell's work-in-progress at Roden Crater, or the works of Robert Smithson and John Heizer, play with desert space on a grand scale. ❧

Above: Morning Promise by Merrill Mahaffey, 1997. Mahaffey strives to capture and comment on the massive forms of Arizona's landscape. His acrylic and watercolor paintings explore evolutionary time, space, and how the earth's colors change in the passage of a day. *Suzanne Brown Galleries, Scottsdale. Left: Quinceañera, Phoenix, Arizona.* Photograph by Louis Carlos Bernal, 1981. *Center for Creative Photography, University of Arizona*

London Bridge Rises Again

Reportedly Arizona's second-biggest tourist attraction (after the Grand Canyon), the venerable London Bridge was bought by millionaire businessman Robert McCulloch, disassembled stone by stone, and brought from England to Lake Havasu in 1971. The lake is man-made, created in the Mojave Desert by the 1938 Parker Dam. The mock British village on its shore is an invention, too.

Starstruck

Founded in 1894 by astronomer Percival Lowell, the Lowell Observatory, near Flagstaff, is one of the world's major research centers. Lowell gained international fame for his theory about a ninth planet; the discovery of Pluto in 1930 (with Lowell's telescope) confirmed his prediction 14 years after his death. Arizona's "other" star-gazer—Kitt Peak National Observatory—is situated atop 6,900-foot Kitt Peak, near Tucson. It contains 21 telescopes, including the most powerful solar telescope ever built.

The Sheltering Skin

A favorite of kitsch lovers everywhere, the Wigwam Village Motel near Holbrook is a beloved emblem of old Route 66. And yes—visitors can still spend the night in one of the stylized, oversized tepees.

Oh, Tumbleweed!

In Chandler, you can attend the Annual Tumbleweed Christmas Tree Lighting Ceremony and watch the lighting of the world's largest (and certainly its only) tumbleweed Christmas tree.

I Brake for Burros

In Oatman, a tiny town on Route 66, the human population hovers around 100. Traffic, such as it is, stops for the other large group of residents: a pack of feral burros that wander freely through town in search of handouts. They're the descendants of pack animals used in Arizona's early 20th-century gold rush.

Teapot for a Tempest

When Phoenix needed to mitigate the impact of a new freeway into the suburbs, it built a concrete noise wall and embellished a five-mile stretch with 35 large-scale works of public art. All are based on vessel forms: some contain misters to refresh walkers; others just make cooling water sounds. The Teapot Gazebo is a fantasy seating area; its spout arches over a bike path.

The Great Indoors

A self-contained artificial environment, Biosphere 2 was modeled by its creators on Biosphere 1 (Earth). Within 3.5 glass-walled acres, it contains replicas of seven ecological areas, including an ocean, a rainforest, a farm, a desert, and a savannah. In 1991 eight people were sealed inside the Biosphere for two years.

Great People

A selective listing of Arizonans, native and adopted, concentrating on the arts.

Maynard Dixon (1875–1946), came to Arizona in the 1890s to paint landscapes and locals; settled in Tucson in 1939

Edward Abbey (1927–1989), eloquent, curmudgeonly scribe of the natural world

Bruce E. Babbitt (b. 1938), descendant of an old Arizona family; served two terms as Arizona governor, 1978–86

Erma Bombeck (1927–1996), household humorist whose column was read by millions

Andy Devine (1905–1977), actor whose birthplace, Kingman, celebrates Andy Devine Days each October

Max Ernst (1891–1976), surrealist painter; built a house in Sedona in the 1940s

Geronimo (1829–1909), famed Apache leader (his real name was Goyahkla)

Barry Morris Goldwater (b. 1909), Phoenix native and U.S. senator; ran for president in 1964

Zane Grey (1872–1939), renowned writer of Western novels, many set in Arizona

Sharlot Hall (1870–1943), writer, poet, and historian; moved to Arizona as a child

Carl Trumbull Hayden (1877–1972), legislator, served a record 57 years in Congress

Helen Hull Jacobs (1908–1997), tennis champion of the 1930s, born in Globe; won Wimbledon singles in 1936

Fred Kabotie (1900–1986), beloved Hopi painter from Shungopavi village

Percival Lowell (1855–1916), came to Arizona in 1893 and founded Lowell Observatory

Lucy Drake Marlow (1890–1978), one of Arizona's first professional women artists

Nampeyo (1859–1942), acclaimed potter; revived traditional colors and designs of Hopi pottery

Sandra Day O'Connor (b. 1930), state senator and jurist, first woman Supreme Court justice

William Hubbs Rehnquist (b. 1924), attorney and judge; named to the Supreme Court in 1971; became chief justice in 1986

Linda Ronstadt (b. 1946), versatile vocalist from old Tucson musical family

Jim Thorpe (1888–1953), attended Carlisle Indian School; Olympic medalist in track

Morris King Udall (b. 1922), born in St. Johns; served 15 terms as a U.S. representative

Stewart Lee Udall (b. 1920), first Arizonan in U.S. cabinet as secretary of the interior, 1961–69

Frank Lloyd Wright (1867–1959), giant among American architects; created Taliesin West in Scottsdale in 1937

...and Great Places

Some interesting derivations of Arizona place names.

Ajo The Tohono O'odham word *au'auho,* meaning "paint." Red pigment used for body paint is found here.

Carefree A planned community near Phoenix; street names include Easy Street, Wampum Way, and Ho and Hum Streets.

Chloride A mining camp in the 1860s, named for the type of silver ore found in the area.

Deadman Flat Named for the discovery of a dead trapper who had shot his own horse, then himself.

Dragoon A town, a mountain pass, and a spring are all named for the U.S. Dragoons.

Globe Town supposedly named for a globe-shaped boulder of almost pure silver.

Gripe A State Agricultural Inspection Point, so named due to disgruntled workers there— or the complaints of motorists forced to stop (or both).

Oracle Named for the ship that brought the nearby Oracle Mine's founder, Albert Weldon.

Phoenix In the 1870s farms, then a town, rose, phoenix-like, from the arid desert.

Pipe Spring Named for a shooting contest involving a Mormon settler's pipe.

Salome Christened in 1904 when Grace Salome Pratt tried to walk barefoot in hot sand and ended up dancing.

Santa Claus A Kingman subdivision designed like a movie set; the developers put everyone who visited on their Christmas card list.

Sedona Named for Sedona M. Schnebly, who, with husband Carl, founded the town in 1902.

Show Low From the card game of Seven-up, played to determine a property claim: "If you can show low, you win."

Skull Valley So-called because the first cavalrymen to ride into the valley found piles of bleached skulls.

Superstition Mountains Site of many legends, including that of the Lost Dutchman mine, still undiscovered.

Total Wreck Ghost town named for a mine site characterized by a litter of boulders.

Weaver's Needle Rock in the Superstition Mountains; may be named after early scout Pauline Weaver.

Why Town grew up in the 1960s at "Y" junction in the road.

Window Rock The tribal capital of the Navajo Nation takes its name from the huge natural window in the sandstone cliffs.

Tombstone Mythic Wild West town and site of a huge silver strike.

ARIZONA BY THE SEASONS
A Perennial Calendar of Events and Festivals

Here is a selective listing of events that take place each year in the months noted; we suggest calling ahead to local chambers of commerce for dates and details.

Ongoing

Tucson Arts District
Art Walk
Late afternoon tours of downtown art spaces. Thursdays year-round, except Thanksgiving.

Downtown Phoenix
Phoenix First Fridays
Self-guided tour of galleries, art spaces, and studios. Monthly Oct–Jun: first Fridays, 7–10 p.m.

January

Litchfield Park
Native American Invitational Fine Arts Festival

Scottsdale
Phoenix Open
Top PGA tour event; world's best golfers tee off.

Barrett-Jackson Auction
World's largest antique/classic car auction.

Tempe
Fiesta Bowl Football Classic
College team playoff on New Year's Day; nationally televised.

Tucson
Southern Arizona Square and Round Dance Festival

Indian America New Year's Competition PowWow & Indian Craft Market

February

Phoenix
Native American Hoop Dance Championship
Top dancers vie for the title of world champion.

Quartzite
PowWow Gem and Mineral Show
Huge gathering in a tiny town; vendors, entertainment.

Scottsdale
Jaycees' Parada del Sol Rodeo
Rodeo and nation's longest horse-drawn parade.

Sedona
International Film Festival

Tubac
Festival of the Arts
Arizona's oldest arts fair.

Tucson
La Fiesta de los Vaqueros
Parade and nation's largest outdoor midwinter rodeo.

Wickenburg
Gold Rush Days
Held for 50 years; features senior rodeo, Western dances.

March

Apache Junction
Lost Dutchman Gold Mine Superstition Mountain Trek

Chinle
Pow Wow Festival
Includes Chinle Agency Navajo Song and Dance.

Phoenix
Heard Museum Guild Indian Fair and Market
More than 300 top artists.

Salt River Reservation
Pima Trade Fair and Dances

Scottsdale
National Festival of the West
Western music, cowboy poetry, cook-off.

Tucson
Chamber Music Festival
Concerts, master classes.
Yaqui Dances and Pageant

Valley of the Sun (Phoenix, Scottsdale, and environs)
Cactus League Baseball
Eight major-league baseball teams play exhibition games.

April

Bisbee
La Vuelta de Bisbee
Nationally recognized bicycle racing event over hills of Bisbee.

Tucson
International Mariachi Conference
Mariachi performances and workshops; largest of its kind.

May

Statewide
Cinco de Mayo celebrations

Flagstaff
Native American Arts and Crafts Festival
Exhibits one weekend each month, May to July.

Jerome
Annual Home Tour
Public tours of the town's many historic houses.

Tombstone
Wyatt Earp Days

June

Flagstaff
Festival of Native American Arts
Runs June through August at the Coconino Center for the Arts.

Prescott
Territorial Days
Rodeo, 10k run, carnival.

San Carlos Reservation, Peridot
Apache Ceremonials

Window Rock
Navajo Nation Treaty Day

July

Flagstaff
Jazz, Rhythm & Blues Festival
Festival of Native American Arts
A juried exhibit representing artists from the Four Corners area; July through Aug.

Flagstaff Festival of the Arts
July and August; features jazz, classical, and chamber music.

Pinetop–Lakeside
Native American Arts and Crafts Festival
Indian artists and crafstmen, storytellers, dancers.

Prescott
Fourth of July Celebration
Includes World's Oldest Rodeo, cowboy golf tournament.

August

Flagstaff
Festival in the Pines
Handweavers Guild Exhibit and Sale

Whiteriver
Apache Fair
Features the Crown Dance

September

Grand Canyon
Chamber Music Festival
Series of evening concerts, from jazz to classical.

Payson
Old-Time Fiddlers' Contest
Fiddlers from all over Arizona compete for state championship.

Sedona
Jazz on the Rocks
Internationally known outdoor jazz festival.

Window Rock
Navajo Nation Fair
One of the largest Native American fairs.

October

Kingman
Andy Devine Days

Phoenix
Arizona State Fair
Cowboy Artists of America Annual Show and Sale
Premier Western art event.

Sedona
Fiesta Del Tlaquepaque
Folklorico dance, mariachis, flamenco guitarists.

Tombstone
Helldorado Days
Shootouts, rodeo, parade.

November

Florence
Florence Junior Parada
For 65 years; world's oldest continous junior rodeo and parade.

Gila River
Native American Art Festival
Features dance, festival, and tribute powwow.

Tohono O'odham Reservation
All-Indian Tribal Fair and Rodeo

December

Lake Powell
Festival of Lights Boat Parade

Sedona
Festival of Lights
Features 4,000 luminarias; entertainment.

Wickenburg
Cowboy Christmas
Singing, crafts, poetry reading.

Window Rock
Christmas Arts and Crafts Fair
Sponsored by the Navajo Nation.

WHERE TO GO
Museums, Attractions, Gardens, and Other Arts Resources

Call for seasons and hours when open.

Museums

AMERIND FOUNDATION MUSEUM
2100 N. Amerind Rd., Dragoon, 520-586-3666
Housed in Spanish Colonial Revival buildings; extensive holdings and exhibits featuring Native American culture, including arts and history.

ARIZONA HISTORICAL SOCIETY MUSEUM
949 E. 2nd St., Tucson, 520-628-5774
Exhibits recount Arizona's cultural history from Spanish Colonial times through the 20th century.

ARIZONA STATE MUSEUM
University of Arizona, Park Ave. and University Blvd., Tucson, 520-621-6302
Enormous holdings concentrate on Native American cultures, from 10,000 B.C. to the present.

ARIZONA–SONORA DESERT MUSEUM
Tucson Mountain Park, 2021 N. Kinney Rd., Tucson, 520-883-1380
One of the 10 best institutions of its kind in the nation, this zoo and garden features 1,300 plant species.

BISBEE MINING AND HISTORICAL MUSEUM
5 Copper Queen Plaza, Bisbee, 520-432-7071
Housed in former mining company headquarters; displays depict life in the mining town; for underground tour, call 520-432-2071.

CENTER FOR CREATIVE PHOTOGRAPHY
University of Arizona, Tucson, 520-621-7968
Outstanding, comprehensive collection (more than 50,000 works, plus reference materials). Changing exhibits feature renowned photographers.

THE HEARD MUSEUM
22 E. Monte Vista Rd., Phoenix, 602-252-8840
World-class collection contains more than 75,000 artifacts and artworks of Native American culture.

JOHN WESLEY POWELL MEMORIAL MUSEUM
6 N. Lake Powell Blvd., Page, 520-645-9496
Dedicated to the explorer of the Grand Canyon.

MUSEUM OF NORTHERN ARIZONA
3101 N. Fort Valley Rd., Flagstaff, 520-774-5211
Exhibits feature the natural and cultural heritage of the Four Corners region.

PHIPPEN MUSEUM
4701 Highway 89 North, Prescott, 520-778-1385
Changing exhibits on art of the American West.

PHOENIX ART MUSEUM
1625 N. Central Ave., Phoenix, 602-257-1222
Southwest's largest art museum, home to a collection from all over the world.

PUEBLO GRANDE MUSEUM
4619 E. Washington St., Phoenix, 602-495-0900
A prehistoric Hohokam mound and village ruins; interpretive exhibits.

SHARLOT HALL MUSEUM
415 W. Gurley St., Prescott, 520-445-3122
Named for one of Arizona's favorite poets; features Arizona historical exhibits, including the original 1864 log governor's mansion.

TUCSON MUSEUM OF ART AND HISTORIC BLOCK
140 N. Main Ave., Tucson, 520-624-2333
Contains pre-Colombian, Spanish Colonial, Western, and folk art. Early Tucson homes are in surrounding district.

Parks and Archeological Sites

CANYON DE CHELLY NATIONAL MONUMENT
P.O. Box 588, Chinle, 520-674-5436
Spectacular rock canyon, home to the Navajo, is restricted to visitors; the White House Ruin is one site accessible without a Navajo guide.

CASA GRANDE RUINS NATIONAL MONUMENT
P.O. Box 518, Coolidge, 520-723-3172
Four-story ruin dates from the 14th century, a prime example of impressive Hohokam architecture.

CHIRICAHUA NATIONAL MONUMENT
Don Cabezas Rt. Box 6500, Willcox, 520-824-3560
Among the wonders of these mountains are dramatic erosion-sculpted rock formations.

GRAND CANYON NATIONAL PARK
Grand Canyon, Arizona, 520-638-7888
The "crown jewel" of Arizona's Canyon Country; may be experienced from either the frequently visited South Rim or the quieter North Rim.

MONTEZUMA CASTLE NATIONAL MONUMENT
P.O.Box 219, Camp Verde, 520-567-3322
Ruins of an ancient pueblo from the Sinagua culture are visible in a huge cave high in a limestone cliff

MONUMENT VALLEY
P.O. Box 93, Monument Valley, Utah, 801-727-3287
Navajo tribal park on the Utah–Arizona border is a marvel of rock formations; can be toured by car in designated areas.

NAVAJO NATIONAL MONUMENT
HC-71 Box 3, Tonalea, 520-672-2366
Arguably the most remarkable of Arizona's prehistoric ruins, Keet Seel (a 160-room pueblo) and Betatakin (135 rooms) can be seen on guided walking tours.

OAK CREEK CANYON
Coconino National Forest, 2323 Greenlaw Ln., Flagstaff, 520-527-7400
Beautiful area features Slide Rock State Park, where swimmers can zoom down a natural rock slide into a pool.

ORGAN PIPE CACTUS NATIONAL MONUMENT
Rt. l, P.O. Box 100, Ajo, 520-387-6849
Only place in the world where these cacti are native.

PETRIFIED FOREST NATIONAL PARK
Petrified National Forest, 520-524-6228
Trunks of trees agatized over centuries are in abundance; another must-see is the Anasazi petroglyphs.

SAGUARO NATIONAL PARK
East unit: 3693 S. Old Spanish Trail, Tucson; West unit: 2700 N. Kinney Rd., Tucson; both 520-296-8576
The densest concentration of cacti is found at the West unit.

SUNSET CRATER VOLCANO NATIONAL MONUMENT
Rt. 3, Box 149, Flagstaff, 520-527-7042
A 1,000-foot cinder cone is what's left of this extinct volcano; its bright reddish rock looks like fire from a distance.

TONTO NATIONAL MONUMENT
HCO2 Box 4602, Roosevelt, 520-467-2421
Only ruin of a prehistoric Sulado pueblo ruin open to the public; near the Roosevelt Dam, also well worth seeing.

TUMACÁCORI NATIONAL MONUMENT
P.O. Box 67, Tumacácori, 520-398-2341
Preserves the abandoned Mission San Jose de Tumacácori.

Attractions

BOYCE THOMPSON ARBORETUM STATE PARK
37615 Highway 60, Superior, 520-689-2811
Thirty-five acres of nature trails take visitors through a forest of desert plants; historic greenhouses exhibit cacti.

CHAPEL OF THE HOLY CROSS
Sedona
Soaring contemporary chapel, built in 1953, set dramatically against Sedona's red rock cliffs.

COSANTI
6433 E. Doubletree Rd., Paradise Valley 602-948-6145
Visionary architect Paolo Soleri designed this village of earth-cast organic forms; another site, Arcosanti, is near Phoenix.

HALL OF FLAME
6101 E. Van Buren, Phoenix, 602-275-3473
Collection of 120 pieces of classic fire equipment and memorabilia.

HOOVER DAM
Hoover Dam Visitor Center, 702-294-3523
One of the highest dams ever constructed (726 feet); guided tours take visitors by elevator down to the power plant.

HUBBELL TRADING POST NATIONAL HISTORIC SITE
On AZ 264, near Keams Canyon, 520-755-3254
The quintessential trading post, founded in 1876 on the Navajo Reservation, and still going strong.

LONDON BRIDGE
Lake Havasu City, 520-855-0888
Brought over from London in 1968, the bridge was reconstructed over a man-made inlet on the Colorado River.

LOWELL OBSERVATORY
1400 W. Mars Hill Rd., Flagstaff, 520-774-2096
Dating from 1894, this famous observatory is where the planet Pluto was discovered; guided tours.

MISSION SAN XAVIER DEL BAC
Rt. ll, Box 645. San Xavier Rd., Tohono O'odham Reservation, 520-294-2624
One of the loveliest Spanish missions; recently restored.

NATIONAL OPTICAL ASTRONOMY OBSERVATORIES–KITT PEAK
950 Cherry Ave., P.O. Box 26732, Tucson, 520-318-8200
Houses the world's largest collection of optical telescopes; daily guided tours.

REX ALLEN ARIZONA COWBOY MUSEUM
155 N. Railroad Ave., Willcox, 520-384-4583
Museum a tribute to TV and film star Rex Allen and Arizona's pioneer ranchers and cowboys.

OLD TUCSON STUDIOS
Tucson Mountain Park, Ajo Way, 520-883-0100
Built by Columbia Pictures as a replica of 1860s Tucson; features Wild West entertainment.

TALIESIN WEST
Shea Blvd., Scottsdale, 602-860-8810
Created by Frank Lloyd Wright in 1937; center for the Frank Lloyd Wright School of Architecture.

ZANE GREY MUSEUM
408 W. Main St., Suite 8, Payson, 520-474-6243
Exhibits of memorabilia, rare books, movie posters, pertaining to this novelist of the West; Western art gallery.

Other Resources

ARIZONA OFFICE OF TOURISM
2762 N. 3rd St., Ste. 4015, Phoenix, 602-230-7733

SCOTTSDALE CENTER FOR THE ARTS
7383 Scottsdale Mall, Scottsdale, 602-994-2787

CREDITS

The authors have made every effort to reach copyright holders of text and owners of illustrations, and wish to thank those individuals and institutions that permitted the reprinting of text or the reproduction of works in their collections. Those credits not listed in the captions are provided below. References are to page numbers; the designations *a, b,* and *c* indicate position of illustrations on pages.

Text

Alfred A. Knopf, Inc.: *The Man Who Walked Through Time* by Colin Fletcher. Copyright © 1967 by Alfred A. Knopf, Inc. By permission of Random House, Inc.

Bantam Doubleday Dell: From *Tombstone: An Iliad of the South West* by Walter Noble Burns. Copyright © 1927, 1929 by Doubleday, a division of Bantam Doubleday Dell Publishing Group, Inc. Used by permission of Doubleday, a division of Bantam Doubleday Dell Publishing Group, Inc.

The Frank Lloyd Wright Foundation: *An Autobiography* by Frank Lloyd Wright. Copyright © 1932, 1943, 1994, 1998 by the Frank Lloyd Wright Foundation, Scottsdale, AZ.

Mountain Press Publishing Company: *Roadside History of Arizona* by Marshall Trimble. Copyright © 1986 by Mountain Press Publishing Company, Missoula, MT.

Thunder Bay Press: *American Southwest: A People and Their Landscape* by Michael Grant. Copyright © 1992 by Thunder Bay Press.

University of Arizona Press: *Secrets from the Center of the World* by Joy Harjo and Stephen Strom. Copyright © 1989 by the Arizona Board of Regents. Excerpt from the poem "Suitcase of Saints" and the poem "Waila Music" from *Ocean Power* by Ofelia Zepeda. Copyright ©1995 by Ofelia Zepeda. *Images and Conversations: Mexican-Americans Recall a Southwestern Past,* text by Patricia Preciado Martin and photographs by Louis Carlos Bernal. Copyright © 1983 by the Arizona Board of Regents. Reprinted by permission of the University of Arizona Press.

University of Oklahoma Press: *Arizona: A Short History* by Odie B. Faulk. Copyright © 1970 by the University of Oklahoma Press.

Illustrations

PETER ADAMS: **46b** *Afternoon Shadows at Maricopa Point.* Oil on board. 18 x 22". ADSTOCK: **70, 78b, 89;** AMERICAN INDIAN CONTEMPORARY ARTS, SAN FRANCISCO: **82b** *Untitled* by Aaron Freeland. Pastel. 29½ x 22"; THE ANSCHUTZ COLLECTION, DENVER: **19** *Grand Canyon.* Oil on canvas. 40 x 30". Photo M. Varon; ARIZONA PEPPER PRODUCTS CO.. **68b** Hot sauce label; ARIZONA HIGHWAYS: **76b** *Arizona Highways* cover; ARIZONA HISTORICAL SOCIETY: **29b, 35b, 39b, 60a, 61a** Mural. Oil on canvas. 31¾ x 73½"; **66b, 79b;** ARIZONA STATE CAPITOL MUSEUM: **37b;** ARIZONA STATE MUSEUM, UNIVERSITY OF ARIZONA: **41b;** ARIZONA THEATER COMPANY: **75a;** BARBARA BASH CALLIGRAPHY & ILLUSTRATION: **68a** Saguaro cooking illustration. 8½ x 11"; TOM BEAN: **50b, 86b&c;** BISBEE MINING AND HISTORICAL MUSEUM: **40;** SUZANNE BROWN GALLERIES, SCOTTSDALE: **18b** *Stages of Bloom.* Oil on canvas. 51 x 76"; **22–23** *The Superstitions.* Oil on canvas. 20 x 64"; **72** *Raging Bull.* Watercolor. 60 x 80"; **82a** *Human Nature at Work in the Cool of the Evening at Ventana Canyon.* Pastel on sanded paper. 20½ x 25½"; **85a** *Morning Promise.* Oil on canvas. 38 x 30"; DAVID BURCKHALTER: **37a, 78c;** BURLINGTON NORTHERN SANTE FE COLLECTION: **28** *A Showery Day, Grand Canyon.* Oil on canvas. 30 x 40"; CANYON RECORDS, PHOENIX: **79a** O'odham album cover; AMON CARTER MUSEUM: **34b** *Walpi, Arizona.* Watercolor and graphite on paper. 17¼ x 13¼"; CENTER FOR CREATIVE PHOTOGRAPHY, UNIVERSITY OF ARIZONA: **85b** *Quinceañera;* CORBIS: **30a, 34a, 56b, 64b, 71b, 73a, 86a;** DON CROWLEY: **47b** *Fry Bread.* Pencil. 17½ x 21½"; DENVER PUBLIC LIBRARY: **16;** DRK PHOTO: **14b, 22a, 27, 69a;** EL POTRERO TRADING POST: **55a;** COLLECTION PATRICK EDDINGTON: **1** Horse with birds, cardboard cutout. Photo Susan Makov; DAVID EMERICK PHOTOGRAPHY: **15b;** DAVID FISCHEL: *Harmony in the Red Rocks.* Graphic relief in wood. 36 x 22"; FOX PHOTOGRAPHY: **64a;** ROBERT FRERK: **20a;** GARLAND'S NAVAJO RUGS, SEDONA: **45b** Pictorial rug. 38 x 42"; JOHN GERLACH: **20b;** GILCREASE MUSEUM, TULSA, OK: **52a** *Fertility Symbols.* Watercolor. 12 x 8½"; GRAND CANYON NATIONAL PARK MUSEUM: **29a;** HARRIES/HEDER COLLABORATIVE: **87a** Teapot wall cycle. Steel. 14 x 7'; THE HEARD MUSEUM, PHOENIX: **33a** Navajo concha belt. 50"; **52b** Hopi kachina dolls, **56a, 83**

Tall Visitor at Tocito. Oil and acrylic. 48 x 60"; HENEBRY PHO-TOGRAPHY: **73b**; HUBBELL TRADING POST NATIONAL HIS-TORIC SITE, GANADO: **32b** *Hosh-Cane-Ah-Sue-It, Navajo.* Conte crayon drawing on paper. 10¾ x 10½". HUTR-1976; **44a** *Untitled.* Oil on canvas. 15¾ x 20¼". HUTR-3457; HUNTER MUSEUM OF ART, CHATTANOOGA, TN: **80** *Arizona Altar.* Oil and pencil on unprimed cotton. 53 x 40½"; LINDA HUSTED: **66a**; IMAGE WORKS: **58b**; INTERNATIONAL MUSEUM OF PHOTOGRAPHY AND FILM, GEORGE EASTMAN HOUSE, ROCHESTER: **43a** *Migratory Cotton Picker.* Gelatin sil-ver print; JERRY JACKA PHOTOGRAPHY: **14a, 24b, 30b&c, 35a, 43b, 44b**; LIBRARY OF CONGRESS: **74a, 75b**; MARION LOCKS GALLERY, PHILADELPHIA: **57** *Lake Powell 2.* Colored pencil on paper. 40 x 60"; LINDA LOMAHAFTEWA: *Animal Keeper.* Monotype. 31½ x 42¼"; LUCY DRAKE MARLOW ART COLLECTION TRUST: **48** *Yaqui Indian Woman.* Oil on canvas. 30 x 38"; McCAIN PHOTOGRAPHY: **13b, 23a, 55b, 63b, 69b**; THE MENIL COLLECTION, HOUSTON: **81a** *Colline Inspirée.* Oil on canvas. 28¾ x 36¼". Photo Paul Hester; MEYER GALLERY: **77b** *Keep Loading, Jenny.* Oil on canvas. 30 x 24"; MINDEN PICTURES: **18a**; MORNING STAR GALLERY: **33b** Navajo serape; VINCENT J. MUSI: **60, 87b&cc**; NATIONAL GEOGRAPHIC IMAGE COLLECTION: **12**; NATIONAL MUSEUM OF AMERICAN ART, SMITHSONIAN INSTITUTION/ART RESOURCE, NY: **8–9** *The Chasm of the Colorado.* Oil on canvas. 84⅜ x 144¾"; **45a** *Two Navajo Men.* Pine board with house paint. 28½ x 4 x 5" and 28 x 13 x 10"; NATIONAL MUSEUM OF THE AMERICAN INDIAN, SMITHSONIAN INSTITUTION: **32a** *Navajo Squaw Dance.* Watercolor on paper board. 22 x 30"; NATIONAL PORTRAIT GALLERY, SMITHSONIAN INSTITU-TION/ART RESOURCE, NY: **77a** *Zane Grey.* Charcoal on paper. 24 x 18"; OAKLAND MUSEUM OF CALIFORNIA: **67b** Spanish wrought-iron gate; PANORAMIC IMAGES: **10, 24a, 26–27, 51a**; JACK PARSONS PHOTOGRAPHY: **59, 62a, 63a, 65b**; GERALD PETERS GALLERY: **47a** *Against the Sunset.* Oil on canvas. 22 x 30"; PHIPPIN MUSEUM, PRESCOTT, AZ: **36b** *Father Kino.* Statue in bronze. 40 x 20 x 21"; **48b** *Yavapai Lands.* Oil on canvas. 7 x 10"; PHOENIX ART MUSEUM: **2** *Cathedral Rock.* Gouache on board. 9⅛ x 6¼". Gift of Dr. F. M. Hinkhouse; **21b** *Chain of Spires along the Gila River.* Oil on canvas. 31 x 42". Museum purchase with funds provided by the estate of Carolanne Smurthwaite. Photo Craig Smith; **25** *Canon de Chelly.* Oil and sand on canvas. 54 x 30". Museum purchase with funds provided by an anonymous donor. Photo Craig Smith; **36a** *Tumacácori Mission.* Oil on canvas. 30 x 46". Gift of Francis Hover Stanley and Carolanne Smurth-waite, by exchange; **41a** *Copper.* Oil on canvas. 38 x 46". Museum purchase with funds provided by Western Art Associates. Photo Craig Smith; PHOENIX ARTS COMMIS-SION: **51b**; PHOTO RESEARCHERS, INC.: **13a**; CHUCK PLACE: **67a**; JAMES PROSEK: **15a** *Apache Trout*; JAMES RANDKLEV: **21a**; FREDERIC REMINGTON ART MUSEUM, OGDENSBURG, NY: **11** *The Rattlesnake.* Cast bronze. 23⅞"; ROCKWELL MUSEUM, CORNING, NY: **42** *The Mix-Up.* Oil on canvas. 30 x 48". Photo Charlie Swain; ROSWELL MUSEUM AND ART CEN-TER, ROSWELL, NM: **54** *Santo.* Oil on canvas. 40 x 28". Gift of Arthur Jonson; JOHN SAMORA: **62b, 65a, 78a**; SHARLOT HALL MUSEUM, PRESCOTT: **48a** *Untitled.* Oil on canvas. 67 x 42"; **76a**; SHOOTING STAR: **39a, 74b**; TONY STONE IMAGES: **71a**; SUPERSTOCK: **38b**; TALIESIN WEST–FRANK LLOYD WRIGHT SCHOOL OF ARCHITECTURE: **58a**; JOY TASH GALLERY: **84** *Suburban Ranchette: Utopian Bliss at the End of the Millennium.* Acrylic on canvas. 40 x 48"; TRUSTEES OF THE ANSEL ADAMS PUBLISHING RIGHTS TRUST: **88** *Maynard Dixon.* Photograph by Ansel Adams; TUCSON ART MUSEUM: **61b**; UNIVERSITY OF OKLAHOMA LIBRARIES, WESTERN HISTORY COLLECTION: **38a**; WALLIS COLLECTION: **13c** Petrified Forest shipping tag; WHITNEY MUSEUM OF AMERICAN ART, NEW YORK: **53** *Hopi Snake Dance, Number I.* Watercolor and graphite on paper. 15 x 12"; THE WITKIN GALLERY, INC., NEW YORK: **31**; WILHELMI-HOLLAND GALLERY, CORPUS CHRISTI, TX: **46a** Ceramic Boots. Earthenware. 15½ x 9"

Acknowledgments

Walking Stick Press wishes to thank our project staff: Miriam Lewis, Joanna Lynch, Kina Sullivan, Thérèse Martin, Laurie Donaldson, Lani Gallegos, Nancy Barnes, and Adam Ling.

For other assistance with Arizona, we are especially grateful to: Laurel Anderson/Photosynthesis, Lindsay Kefauver/Visual Resources, Ed Chamberlain at the Hubbell Trading Post NHS, Lucy Jane Jackson, Ed McCain, Norm Tessman at the Sharlot Hall Museum, Faulkner Color Lab, and the staff of the Arizona Histori-cal Society.